INVADED BY GOD

MYSTICISM AND THE INDWELLING TRINITY

by

GEORGE A. MALONEY, S.J.

DIMENSION BOOKS

DENVILLE, NEW JERSEY

Imprimi Potest: Rev. Vincent M. Cooke, S.J.
Provincial of the New York Province
February 1, 1979

DEDICATION

To the Southern California Renewal Communities of Los Angeles under the direction of Rev. Ralph T. Tichenor, S.J.

ACKNOWLEDGEMENTS

Sincere thanks to Mrs. Rita Ruggiero for typing this manuscript; to Andrea Federoff, Sister Francoise O'Hare, RSHM, and to Sister Joseph Agnes, S.C.H. for their careful reading and correcting of the manuscript and for other suggestions that proved most helpful. A special thanks to Jim and Lou Anne Dunn for making it possible for me to stay in their hermitage to write this book. Grateful acknowledgement is made to the following publishers: Darton, Longman & Todd, Ltd., and Doubleday & Company, Inc., N.Y., for excerpts from *The Jerusalem Bible,* copyright 1966 by Darton, Longman & Todd, Ltd., and Doubleday and Company, Inc. All scriptural texts are from this Bible version unless otherwise noted.

TABLE OF CONTENTS

INTRODUCTION

I often think: what would Jesus Christ say to us if He returned to this earth again in human form and walked into some of our Christian churches on any given Sunday? Would he complain that there is too much talk about money from the pulpit? Too many committee meetings and cake sales? Would He find the sermons preached too much of a head trip with little said about experiencing the God of love in prayer and our being love to one another in daily life? Surely He would smile at how organized His Churches have become. Or would He weep?

All of these things are peripheral to Jesus Christ. I feel He would ask, however, one, principal question. "What ever happened to My revelation about My Father and Me coming to dwell in you through our Spirit of love?" He would complain, I feel sure, that the life He came to bring us has become diluted, a drop of water, taken from a torrential waterfall, and placed in a stopped-up test-tube. "I came to give you life, that you might have it more abundantly" (Jn 10:10). This life was to be an on-going process of knowing and loving, of *experiencing* profoundly the Father and the Son in their Spirit.

And eternal life is this:
to know you,
the only true God,
and Jesus Christ whom you have sent (Jn 17:3).

Christianity was meant by Jesus to be a living experience of *being in* the trinitarian community, loved infinitely by the Father in His Son, Jesus Christ, through his Holy Spirit. In the earlier centuries of Christianity theology was a mysticism about the indwelling Trinity, living within and transforming Christians into divinized children of God. It was a consciously experienced participation in God's life. Theologians were the purified ascetics who, pure in heart, were caught up in the nonobjectified, mysterious, circular movement of triadic love. They were taught a knowledge of God that was not different from experienced love of God. And they taught, not by relaying to others a system of abstract truths about God, but by leading other Christians into the mystery of God.

A THEOLOGICAL MYSTICISM

Theology for St. Maximus the Confessor was *theoria theologica,* the contemplation of the Trinity within the Christian mystic and without, in the world about him. It was meant to be practical. The Greek Fathers felt that this was the end of our human existence: to live experientially in the transforming love of the Father, Son and Spirit so as to be transformed into love for the world. The beginning and the end, the Alpha and the Omega for such mystical theologians was the Holy Trinity.

But how different is our concept of theology and theologians today! When speculative theology became divorced from mysticism, the doctrine of the Trinity was something taught, to which Christians gave an intellectual assent and accepted as true. It was not presented as most practical, having transforming effects on our concepts of ourselves, of God, of the Church and of the world.

In fact in his book on the Trinity, Karl Rahner complains that, if this doctrine were to be declared unnecessary to the Christian faith, few Christian lives would be affected, and sadly enough Rahner writes: ". . . the major part of religious literature could well remain virtually unchanged."

Most preachers will admit that the most difficult topic to preach about is the Trinity. Our Western mind has developed well its ability to objectivize and systematize facts of life into categories of knowledge that can easily be learned. But how does one objectivize such impractical truths as three persons in one nature? How can we understand that these three persons live within us?

AN APOPHATIC APPROACH

This book draws insights from Holy Scripture, the Eastern Fathers and the mystics of all ages to offer a vision of God as invading Love. At the heart of all reality is the Trinity, a loving community of an *I-Thou* in a *We*-family. I have sought to avoid objectivizing the Father, Son and Spirit into a tritheism of three distinct and separate Gods, by appealing to the *apophatic* theology at the heart of Eastern Christian experience. This is not a *negative* theology that would insist we can truly know nothing about God. It denies the power of the human intellect to comprehend God in His ultimate make-up, but it positively insists that for the "poor in spirit" the Kingdom of God is a living experience. For those who mourn shall be comforted and the pure of heart really can "see" God. In a word, to the repentant, the humble ones, who, like children, know their utter dependence upon another for their being, God truly does reveal Himself, but in mystery.

CALL TO MYSTICISM

I have approached the mystery of the Trinity as a dynamic movement of God toward us through His two hands, in the words of St. Irenaeus, Jesus Christ and the Holy Spirit. God's purpose in creating us is that we may share in His very own family life. God's revelation shows us that we can both "know" and experience this mystery. As Christians we are all called to this. We are all, therefore, called to experience that indwelling trinitarian life, which, among the Eastern Fathers, is the essence of Christian mysticism: the love of God in us that differentiates even as it unites.

After developing the mystery of the Trinity, relying on the writings of the early Fathers I have sought to explain the difference between Godhead and Father, and the inter-personal relationships between the Father and the Son in the Holy Spirit. These inter-trinitarian relationships are seen as the basis for God's *essential* relationships to us and to the created world in His uncreated energies of love, which still maintain analogous, personal relationships of Father, Son and Spirit to us as individuals.

The indwelling personal relationships we enjoy with the Son, and differently with the Holy Spirit, are developed. The summary of the book is contained in the last chapter, entitled, "Communion with the Holy Trinity." This Chapter seeks to develop the mystery of the Eucharist as the climax of God's trinitarian self-giving to us and in concluding reminds us that we must be one with the trinitarian community as we become Eucharist to the world.

I ask the indulgence of the reader if this presentation does not always show the clarity and precision of most books treating of the Trinity. This has been my humble attempt to try a different approach to mystery, to mystical theology, as we find it in the Gospel and in the early patristic tradition. If this book should arouse in any reader a greater desire to experience more intimately God the "consuming fire" (Heb. 12:29), the indwelling Trinity living within him or her as in a temple, then my efforts will be greatly rewarded and the Blessed Trinity greatly honored.

George A. Maloney, S.J.

Epiphany, 1979

1

Call to Mysticism

The Grail Legend, written centuries ago by Chretien de Troyes, is about the Holy Grail, the chalice used by Jesus at the Last Supper. It is kept in a castle in the care of a king, called the Fisher King. The king, however, had been severely wounded in his adolescence and lies on a litter. He had been promised by the court fool in prophecy that he would be healed by the Grail when an innocent fool comes to the castle.

Most of us have followed in story book form Parsifal, the hero of the story, all through his many wanderings and heroic adventures. Parsifal, if he asks the right question: "Whom does the Grail serve?" would be able to heal the king. But alas, he forgets the question upon first meeting the king. After more wanderings, Parsifal on Good Friday goes to confession, is reconciled to God and remembers the right question. He sets off for the castle. However, this is where the author decided to end the story.

Down through the ages authors have made attempts to finish the story. One attempt has Parsifal asking the right question: "Whom does the Grail serve?" The answer is given: "The Grail serves the Grail King." He has lived in the central room of the castle from time immemorial. The sick king of the castle is healed at once and all his people live in peace and joy.[1]

Most of us human beings live our lives in search of the Grail. We see it as a goal that will bring us happiness. But we all too often forget the right question. The Grail is not to serve our self-centered desires, our blinded values that we feel will bring us complete happiness. When we can forget our own petty interests and pursuits, in the silence of our own clamorings for instant happiness, we can then ask the right question. We shall learn that the Grail does not exist for us but solely for the Grail King.

SELF-FULFILLMENT

Like Parsifal, we are lonely pilgrims with a quest. We burn with the thirst to become complete, whole, integrated persons. We travel through life's experiences, looking for happiness. Something in us pushes us onward in our quest, something always gnawing at the core of our being, leaving us unfulfilled. We try the pleasures of this world like a child who gleefully stretches out to grasp the glittering soap bubbles. But we stand on the brink of despair clutching a handful of nothingness.

We think honors, wealth and power can bring an end to that inner *malaise*. Perhaps learning or professional work or involvement in social causes can bring those inner yearnings to satisfying fulfillment. Yet like King Solomon we, too, can readily admit:

I then reflected on all that my hands had achieved and on all the effort I had put into its achieving. What vanity it all is and chasing of the wind! (Qo 2:11).

For most of us it takes several years of such futile searching to realize that nothing in the whole world can ever satisfy us but God. For it is God who has given us this basic drive to possess Him and to be possessed by Him. Never on earth has there been a human being who found full self-actualization in the possession of material things or even in the love for individual human beings. This is the way God created man and woman—to find themselves in relation to other knowing and loving beings. And through such love relationships we are to discover the loving beauty of God Himself.

In surrendering to another and ultimately to God in unselfish love, man reaches the highest stage of communication. Through faith in prayer man *knows* God's personal love for him. He can move himself towards Beauty itself, towards the Absolute, the transcendent God, who comes to him in a tender but infinite love. St. Augustine kept searching for the Grail to bring him happiness while all the time the Grail King lived in the center of his heart. Finally, he became convinced that God was the ultimate answer to meaningful existence. He had discovered that the Grail did not exist to bring him happiness, but that it existed, as St. Augustine himself existed, to serve the King who lived in the inner mansion of his own heart.

> Too late have I loved Thee, O Thou, Beauty of ancient days, yet ever new! Too late I loved Thee! And behold, Thou wert within and I abroad, and there I searched for Thee; deformed, I plunging amid those fair forms which Thou hast made. Thou wert with me, but I was not with Thee, which unless they were in Thee, were not at all.[2]

THIRST FOR GOD

God has made us human beings according to His image and likeness (Gn 1:26). We are destined to grow in greater knowledge and love of Him. His loving presence as personalized relations of uncreated energies of love surrounds us, permeates us, bathes us constantly in His great loving communication of Himself to us. This is an ongoing self-giving on the part of God the Father through His Son in His Spirit.

As we become present in knowledge and love to God's loving presence, the seeds that God planted in us gradually grow to fulfillment. We are being driven into the silent desert of our hearts to receive God's Word who will reveal our true dignity to be with Him children of God (Rm 8:15; Ga 4:6). In such silence and inner poverty, we "hear" God's Word. Emil Brunner describes this call to existence:

> The being of man as an 'I' is being from and in the Divine 'Thou,' or more exactly, from and in the Divine Word, whose claim 'calls' man's being into existence.[3]

God is always calling us to consent to be swept up into the Trinitarian life and we alone can reply. Our answer fulfills the purpose for which we were made or we destroy ourselves as human persons. This "existential longing" to be what God wants us to be, in knowing and loving communication with Him, is a spiritual thirst that is at the heart of being truly human. It is a yearning to become "whole" and fulfilled. It is a longing that the image of God in man reach its full fruition.

Many human beings thirst for God only when they have fallen to the depths of human degradation and frustration. Others thirst for God because through the gift of prayer God has revealed Himself in a partial vision of His perfect beauty along with a vivid experience of their own emptiness apart from God. With the Levite in exile we too can cry out in our soul's thirsting for God:

> As a doe longs
>> for running streams,
> so longs my soul
>> for you, my God.
>
> My soul thirsts for God,
>> the God of life;
> when shall I go to see
>> the face of God?
>
> I remember, and my soul
>> melts within me:
> I am on my way to the wonderful Tent,
>> to the house of God,
> amid cries of joy and praise
>> and an exultant throng.
>
> Deep is calling to deep
>> as your cataracts roar;
> all your waves, your breakers,
>> have rolled over me.
>
> In the daytime may Yahweh
>> command his love to come,
> and by night may his song be on my lips,
>> a prayer to the God of my life (Ps 42:1-4, 7-8).

And God promises that to those who thirst He will pour out His life-giving water. "For I will pour out water on the thirsty soul, streams on the dry ground. I will pour my spirit on your descendants, my blessing on your children" (Is 44:3). And God promises: "I will give water from the well of life free to anybody who is thirsty" (Rv 21:6).

St. Gregory of Nyssa builds a spirituality around this biblical concept of "stretching out" always to supersede one's longing so that man is continually searching for greater communication with God, for greater intimacy and deeper union, greater possession of the Unpossessable that makes all other possession vain, to paraphrase the words of the poet, Francis Thompson in his *Hound of Heaven.* By wanting to surpass the attained level of union with God, the spiritual man pushes himself to new desires of self-fulfillment. In his classic on Christian mysticism: *Life of Moses,* St. Gregory writes about this basic yearning or interior "stretching" out to possess God more and more intimately:

> Made to desire and not to abandon the transcendent height by the things already attained, it makes its way upward without ceasing, ever through its prior accomplishments renewing its intensity for the flight. Activity directed toward virtue causes its capacity to grow through exertion; this kind of activity alone does not slacken its intensity by the effort, but increases it.[4]

PRAYER — KEY TO TRANSCENDENCE

Prayer is the art whereby we human beings communicate with God in knowledge and love. We lift our minds and our hearts towards God. But more, we pray, not primarily to receive gifts from God, but to surrender as a self-giving gift to Him, Jesus Christ, who has given us everything. Prayer is our avenue to enter into God's timeless and infinite, personal and perfect love for each of us individually. Prayer raises our consciousness to the primal experience that is the beginning and the end of all reality, namely, being grasped by God, known and loved uniquely by Him so that in such a re-creating experience, we rise to new levels of spiritual perfection.

St. Paul described it as the putting on of the "new man": "Your mind must be renewed by a spiritual revolution, so that you can put on the new self that has been created in God's way, in the goodness and holiness of the truth" (Ep 4:23-24).

Such communication in being should be our most "natural" act, the one that most brings us into the most sublime, inter-personal relationships with God who is all-perfect. As we experience God, not only outside of us in His wondrous creations of nature, but, above all, as inhabiting within us, our response in self-surrendering love pushes our consciousness of our new identity with God to new heights.

It is an exciting, *total* experience that retains much from our past prayerful knowing and loving God. Yet each prayerful encounter, due to the increase in awareness of our *I-ness* toward the *Thou-ness* in God, allows us to enter into a fresh, new experience. Such an expansion of self-identity and inner nobility, due to God's personal love for us, is never content with one such prayerful experience. An inner dynamism, the indwelling Holy Spirit, drives us to continued and more intense relationships.

Love has that quality of the old, the permanent, the stable and the security and complacency that we enjoy in encountering the same source of beauty and joy. Yet the sameness and stability of our love for God fill us with a restless motion, a stretching-out quality towards God, the unpossessable, that thrills us because we know that, try as we may, we can never exhaust this richness. Love always beckons us to partake of more of the joy that is already ours.[5]

EXPERIENCING THE INDWELLING TRINITY

If God is love that knows no end of self-giving, then He is always giving Himself to us in His uncreated energies of love. How amazing to realize that prayer is tuning in to God's eternal, unchanging love for us. We go to prayer not to beg God to love us more. We pray in order to come into the reality of God's eternal love, made into human communication by His Word Incarnate, Jesus Christ.

> God's love for us was revealed
> when God sent into the world his only Son
> so that we could have life through him;
> this is the love I mean:
> not our love for God,
> but God's love for us when he sent his Son
> to be the sacrifice that takes our sins away (1 Jn 4:9-10).

We pray in order to receive the truth from the Holy Spirit of Jesus Christ that convinces us that we are loved infinitely by the Father who loves us in His only begotten Son. "The Spirit himself and our spirit bear united witness that we are children of God. And if we are children we are heirs as well: heirs of God and coheirs with Christ, sharing his sufferings so as to share his glory" (Rm 8:16-17).

We pray in order to be divinized into participators of

God's own nature (2 P 1:4). This is done by God the Father communicating His divine nature to us "through His two hands, Jesus Christ and His Holy Spirit," as St. Irenaeus of the 2nd century wrote. The Good News is that the Kingdom of God is within us. This Kingdom is a knowing and loving relationship, a sharing on our part, through grace, of the Trinity's very own nature along with the particular individual personhood of each person of the Trinity.

Jesus had promised such an indwelling relationship between Him and His Heavenly Father and the individual disciple that keeps His commandments.

> If anyone loves me he will keep my word,
> and my Father will love him,
> and we shall come to him
> and make our home with him (Jn 14:23).

He had promised also to send His Advocate, the Holy Spirit, who would come and abide also with His followers (Jn 14:26; 15:26; Jn 16:7-8). The Holy Spirit, sent into our hearts by the Father through Jesus Christ, comes to seize us and take possession of us in order to give us to the Son. The Son leads us to the Father dwelling along with Him in our hearts. The riches of the mystery of God are inexhaustible, like an abyss. For who of us could ever plumb the depths of God's infinite love, abiding within us? As we begin to contemplate under the guidance of the Holy Spirit the depths of the beauties and the love of the indwelling Trinity, Father, Son and Holy Spirit, we begin to experience what St. Paul meant when he wrote:

> Out of his infinite glory, may he give you the power through His Spirit for your hidden self to grow strong, so

that Christ may live in your hearts through faith, and then, planted in love and built on love, you will with all the saints have strength to grasp the breadth and the length, the height and the depth; until, knowing the love of Christ, which is beyond all knowledge, you are filled with the utter fullness of God (Ep 3:16-19).

To pray is to become conscious of the ever new relationships between the Father, Son and Holy Spirit and the individual, praying. It is to let ourselves enter into the very movement of triadic life living within us. It is to swim in the powerful current of God's uncreated energies of love that completely surround us and permeate us as the ocean saturates a sponge. In such experiential prayer of the heart, we should not stop with mere feelings or affections or thoughts. We have the courage as the Spirit prompts us to pray in Him to move beyond pictures, images and even words. The Fathers of the desert constantly exhort us, as St. Gregory of Sinai summarizes it, "to force your mind to descend from the head to the heart and hold it there."[6]

Prayer becomes more and more a waiting in silence, a listening, a surrendering to the Holy Spirit who brings us to God's Word that gives us knowledge that is beyond human knowledge, that brings us into darkness that is luminous. Only the Holy Spirit can reveal to us an experience of this divine triadic love. God is love (1 Jn 4:8) and this means that He is a community of loving Persons. His very being, His existence is to love. For God, to be is to love. This means that God is constantly leaving Himself to give Himself to and to exist in Another. Each person of the Trinity exists in relationship toward Another. God is Father in relationship to the Son. The Son exists and lives only in and for the Father to whom He gives Himself entirely. Their mutual love expresses itself in a procession of Personified love, the Holy Spirit. To pray in the heart is to experience this immense circulation of love among the Persons within the divine family, drawing us into that same community of love.

A PROFOUND MYSTERY

The mystery of the Trinity is the greatest of all mysteries. It escapes our own human reason and understanding. We can understand somewhat the doctrine of the Incarnate Word for we possess, as Jesus, a human nature. We can understand some of the attributes of God because we have experienced similar perfections in ourselves and in the material creatures around us. But to imagine the one nature of the Godhead as the equally shared essence of three persons, as the dogma of the Trinity is described, is beyond our sense knowledge.

And yet we can both "know" and experience this mystery through God's revelation. Accent should not be placed so much on the difficulty to comprehend this mystery (which then removes the mystery from any relevance to our concrete lives) but rather on the truth that this is a part of God's *mysteries,* His secrets that He reveals to His children so that they may share in His eternal life (Rm 16:25-27; Ep 1:3-14).

Jesus had declared eternal life in terms of knowing: "And eternal life is this: to know you, the only true God, and Jesus Christ whom you have sent" (Jn 17:3). Through God's Word Incarnate, therefore, the One "nearest the heart of the Father" (Jn 1:18), God reveals to us His inner life. This revealing Word, Jesus Christ, by His death and resurrection, is now a living Word, dwelling within us along with His Holy Spirit. He not only gives us the elements that constitute God's inner life but He makes it possible through His Spirit that those elements can be experienced by us.

Thus this trinitarian reality is to be experienced now. The doctrine of the Trinity is not only what makes Christianity uniquely different from all other religions, but it is a reality that effects the fulfillment of our very being as human persons. Christology and all other dogmas, Liturgy and the sacraments, preaching the Gospel and developing the Christian life of Christ-like virtues all have their meaning and subordination to this central teaching of the Trinity.

We are baptized in the Father, Son and Spirit. We profess in faith that, even as infants, we were receiving God's trinitarian actions upon us. We are confirmed, reconciled to God, ordained, married, healed in the name of the three Divine Persons. We bless ourselves in the Trinity and seek to do all for the glory of the Trinity.

God revealed this mystery to us in order that He might humbly share the secret of His own intimate life. This reality is meant to be a living experience for us. We are to live in this teaching. But unfortunately for too many centuries the precisions of professional theologians dominated our approach to the Trinity. We were not rooted in Holy Scripture, God's living Word, who alone can reveal to us this awesome reality and make it effective and transformative in our lives.

We lost contact with the patristic tradition that theologized out of a living mysticism. Such early mystics were the ones, like Sts. Basil, Gregory Nazianzus, Gregory of Nyssa, Athanasius and Cyril of Alexandria, Maximus the Confessor and Symeon the new Theologian, who not

only outlined the element of this dogma but preached it as
the basis of all reality. In their doctrine of divinization
(*theosis*), they boldly proclaimed, in the words of St.
Irenaeus, that God became man in order "that man might
possess the Word, receive adoption and become the son of
God."[7]

For these early Fathers God as Trinity is the ground of
man's being. Man has been created by God's ever constant, never changing, present-now act of love through His
uncreated energies of love. All three Persons act as one in
loving man; yet each Person partakes of the same relational "action toward man as He does within the Trinity
itself. God's personal relationships within the Trinity are
the basis for the "economic" or salvific historical
relatedness of the three Persons toward the human race.
Man never lives outside of the glow of this love. God is
constantly ordering man towards a personal response of
"yes" to God's invitation and involving love that man may
become like to the Image that the Divine Son is.

Thus the revelation of the trinitarian doctrine in Holy
Scripture and the patristic preaching present this mystery
as of most practical consequences for Christians seeking
perfection. And for us also the Christian life should be
seen as a sharing, even now, in the trinitarian life as we
grow in greater awareness of the three Persons in their u-
nique roles to bring us into their divine life. We will develop
at length in subsequent chapters the particular, personal
relationship of each Person to us.

MYSTICISM

Mysticism is one of the most misunderstood words in
the Christian vocabulary. For St. Paul the mystic
(*mystikos* in Greek) was the dynamic Christian who by the

Holy Spirit lived on an integrated level of God's loving presence, both outside of man and within him. He was fundamentally a "spirit-minded" person seeing God at the heart of matter. And true this is. The Christian's end of his life is to contemplate God in all things, because there is precisely where God is.

St. Augustine encourages us

> . . . to understand God, if we are able and as far as we are able, as good without quality, great without quantity, a creator without indigence, ruling but from no position, containing all things without 'having' them, totally everywhere without place, eternal without time, making things that are changeable without change of Himself, and not being subject to the influence of anything.[8]

We are made, not only to adore the transcendent God outside of ourselves by keeping His commandments, but also to enter within ourselves, to go into our "heart," as Holy Scripture describes the deepest levels of our spiritual faculties, and there to adore and surrender in love to God. Mysticism in the Christian sense is the take-over by the Holy Spirit through an ever increasing infusion of faith, hope and love that brings the individual into a greater oneness with the Blessed Trinity dwelling within the Christian contemplative as well as dwelling and operating in all things external to the individual. Growth in prayer is always a process of growth in consciousness of the abiding sense and presence of God and His ever increasing assimilating activities through His love for us. It is a basic standing in a "gaze" before God. We no longer pray with one faculty of our being nor are we content to focus upon one facet of God's being. Our whole being is absorbed into the Being of

God. There is a growing experience of being "begotten" as the Word, the Son of God, is begotten by the Father.

There is also an active response of love through the Spirit as we seek in our daily lives to live on this unitive level of "oneness" with God in all things.

Because of the depths of "personalism" involved, we become more receptive to God's activities in our contemplative prayer. Prayer takes on an attitude of listening to God with the fullness of our being. "Be it done unto me according to Thy Word" (Lk 1:38). More and more we become aware of God's personal gift of His very inner trinitarian life, the Father giving Himself to us through His Son in His Holy Spirit. We are aware that we cannot reach this level of being gifted by God of Himself through our own powers. No one can teach this to us. Only God can reveal such a level of His being our total source of existence.

Mystical contemplation is, therefore, not a conversation with words between ourselves and God but it is life lived on its deepest level. It is an immersion, an assimilation into God's very being. And yet this state of being in God at the deepest center of our being makes us conscious of God's same presence in, surrounding and penetrating all other things. God becomes no longer an object far away or a vague concept. He becomes a dynamic, creative force as He calls at each moment the individual Christian into being as well as offering to the Christian an opportunity to co-create the world according to God's mind.

IS MYSTICISM FOR ALL?

If we conceive the Christian life as growth in knowledge and love of God, then we should also see that mysticism, which embraces the advanced stages of such knowledge and love, should not be something reserved for an elite but it should be the goal of all human beings. And yet for the ordinary person mysticism connotes something that touches demonology, occultism, magic or at most it is given only to a few persons like the saints, gifted enough to have received ecstasies, visions or other spiritual graces.

All too often certain theologians in times past have accentuated the total gratuitousness of mysticism as God's gift for which man can do little to attain. It is true that it is a gift but everything, St. James tells us (Ja 1:17), is gift that comes down to us from the Father of lights. Jesus Christ in the Gospel calls all of us to be perfect as His Heavenly Father is perfect. By our Baptism we are called into that very life of the Trinity. Hence those seeds of a life in God are meant by God's designs to be actuated in ever increasing oneness with God. From Scripture we are to pray always, as St. Paul tells us (1 Th 5:17). Such a state of being present to God always should not be an exceptional state for Christians opened only to a few but it should be the goal of all of our strivings as through prayer and work we cooperate with God's grace to fructify that Divine Life given to us in Baptism and the other sacraments.

The Church has exhorted all of us to perfection. Yet, without a state of habitual remembrance of God's presence and a readiness to love God in all things at all times, there can be little perfection in the Christian life. We see that the Church has canonized some very ordinary persons like St. Benedict Joseph Labre, a beggar, and St. Frances of Rome, a wife and mother, and has approved of their heroic prayer-life as a goal attainable by grace and cooperation even in a quite-ordinary state of life. To love

God and neighbor with our whole heart and whole soul
and whole mind and whole strength ought not to be for a
few extraordinary Christians but should be attainable for
all. Yet such perfect love is what true contemplation and
mysticism are really all about.

God abides in us (Jn 14:21, 23, 26); therefore we
should be able progressively more and more to be aware of
this indwelling presence of the Trinity. Such listening and
surrendering to the indwelling Spirit that dwells within us
(1 Co 3:16; 6:19) as in a temple are essential to contemplation and thus should be also available to all Christians who
seek such an advanced state of oneness with God. God
stands at the door of our hearts and knocks to gain admis-
sion (Rv 3:20) but we must open the door.

Therefore we do not see anything in Scripture that
would teach mysticism as a state for only a few persons. It
is another fact, and regrettable at that, that so few Christians do advance to such maturity in the Christian life. The
fact that the majority of acorns never become fully
developed oak trees does not deny the reality that the
potential is within each acorn to so develop. But Scripture
on every page has God offering Himself in loving union
with His children. This is the abundant life that Jesus
Christ came to give all of us (Jn 10:10).

The Church through its councils and teachers,
especially in the patristic age, has never taught anything
but a universal call to a growth in continued, loving surrender to God's dominance. This is especially seen in the
common teaching among the Greek Fathers concerning
their doctrine that every human being has been created according to God's image and likeness, that is Jesus Christ,
and that Christian perfection is a process of actuating the
seeds of divine life (called *theosis*) through a greater know-

ing and loving *synergy* (a working together) between man and God. St. Gregory the Great gives us the common teaching that the grace of contemplation is available to all persons, regardless of their state of life.

It is not the case that the grace of contemplation is given to the highest and not given to the lowest; but often the highest, and often the most lowly, and very often those who have renounced, and sometimes also those who are married, receive it. If therefore there is no state of life of the faithful, from which the grace of contemplation can be excluded, anyone who keeps his heart within him may also be illumined by the light of contemplation; so that no one can glory in this grace as if it were singular. It is not the high and preeminent members of holy Church only that have the grace of contemplation; but very often those members receive this gift, who, although by desire they already mount to the heights, are still occupying low positions, Almighty God impours the light of contemplation into those who appear to be lowly in the eyes of men, but secretly give themselves up to the pursuit of divine wisdom, pant after heavenly things, and think on the everlasting joys.'

Therefore, we can safely say that all who live the Beatitudes as preached by Jesus Christ, especially those who are poor in spirit and ready to surrender themselves totally to Christ, the clean of heart, will "see" God in varying degrees of contemplation. Historically, however, we can see reasons why certain teachers in the Church taught a contrary doctrine. The greatest factor for de-emphasizing mysticism as the goal of the Christian life, perhaps the greatest, consisted in the over-cautious attitude of such leaders to aberrations that developed among cer-

tain groups, including certain lay "mystics" from the 14th
until the 18th centuries. Some of these excesses are labelled
illuminism, subjectivism and quietism. The great hunger of
the 14th century for mysticism, launched by the writings and
preaching of Meister Eckhart, Tauler, Suso, Ruysbroeck,
Julian of Norwich, Hilton, Rolle, the anonymous author
of the Cloud of Unknowing, the accent given to mysticism
by the lay movements of the Flemish Beguines and
Beghards, the notorious witch hunts and finally the
quietism of Madame Guyon and her followers all com-
pounded to develop among the teaching section of the
Church a great reaction against any type of prayer that
went beyond a discursive level of meditating on the
mysteries of the Gospel. The Jesuits were very instru-
mental through their schools, writings and preaching of
retreats in developing the discursive type of prayer almost
exclusively to the neglect of any more advanced, mystical
prayer.

DIVISIONS OF MYSTICISM

If mysticism, therefore, is a living experience of God
through knowledge and love by which God no longer is encountered as an object outside of us, but as an encom-
passing power of permeating love, we can readily see that
there will be varying degrees of mysticism. The openness to
the Allness of God is attained in a gradual process of communion that unfolds in the ever-deepening silencing of our
own inordinate desires and sense of independence and in
the surrendering of ourselves to God's divine will. This is
at the heart of the Gospel message of death and resurrection and of putting on Jesus Christ, the Way that leads us
to the Father. It is not what can be described in words, but

what must be experienced, that is important.

Evelyn Underhill in a rather well-known definition of mysticism that would apply to all religions defines it thus:

> Mysticism is the expression of the innate yearning of the human spirit towards total harmony with the transcendental order, whatever may be the theological formula in which this order is expressed. This yearning with the great mystics gradually takes possession of the whole field of consciousness; it dominates their whole life and attains its climax in that experience called mystic union, whether it be with God of Christianity the World soul of pantheism or the Absolute of philosophy. This desire for union and straining towards it in as much as they are vital and real (not purely speculative) constitute the real subject of mysticism. Through this the human consciousness reaches its further and richest development. (10)

For St. Francis de Sales, the art of contemplation is a loving, simple and permanent attentiveness of the mind to divine things. It is an experience through knowledge and love given the individual Christian through the infused gifts of the Holy Spirit of faith, hope and love of the abiding loving presence of God as one and yet a community of three loving Persons transforming the Christian into a sharer of that very same divine life. This communion is progressively felt to be a union through assimilation, a continued surrendering of the one possessed to the loving power of God the Possessor. It is a leaving behind of the operations of the senses, emotions and intellectual powers in order to "strain upwards in unknowing as far as may be towards the union with Him who is above all being and knowledge. For by unceasing and absolute withdrawal from thyself and all things in purity, abandon all and set free from all, thou wilt be borne up to the ray of the divine Darkness that surpasses all being."[11]

Most readers are familiar with the terms "acquired" and "infused" contemplation. These are found in most traditional books that treated mysticism from a scholastic framework of philosophy and theology.

Acquired contemplation was supposed to be available to all, achieved by ordinary grace and one's own efforts. It also referred to the type of prayer that was a simplification of one's discursive and affective powers to bring one into a "prayer of simplicity" or the "prayer of simple regard." Often it consisted of a simple word of centering upon the presence of the Lord, repeating that word with a simple regard of faith looking upon the inner presence of the Lord.

Infused contemplation was supposed to be real mysticism, a sheer gift, not given to everyone but only to very special persons. It was a special call, admitting certain stages that were usually defined by the signs that accompanied that level of mysticism, such as Prayer of Quiet, Full Union, Ecstatic Union and Spiritual Marriage.[12] Such stages of mysticism were characterized by an inability to pray discursively, a longing for silence and solitude and an obscure sense of God's presence.

Often certain mystical gifts were manifested in these stages and hence a distinction was made between the "concomitant phenomena" and "charismatic phenomena" of infused contemplation. The first set of gifts was centered around the gifts of the Spirit, especially wisdom and knowledge, deep inward peace, joy, love and the obscure sense of God's presence. The charismatic phenomena were visions, *ESP* powers such as telepathy, clairvoyance, levitation, psychokinesis etc., trances, locutions and ecstasies. These were not considered essential and could be found outside Christianity.

It should be noted that the Greek Fathers never approached mysticism from such an angle, as will be pointed out, and several modern authors such as Karl Rahner also do not hold such a distinction between acquired and infused contemplation. For them all grace is "special," being in essence the self-communication of God.[13] Rahner thus writes:

> Mysticism . . . . occurs within the framework of normal graces and within the experience of faith. To this extent, those who insist that mystical experience is not specifically different from the ordinary life of grace (as such) are certainly right.[14]

M. Raymond gives the distinction between "mystical life" and "mystical prayer." All of us, he claims, are called to the mystical life, but not all are called to the "extraordinary" state of mystical prayer.[15] The mystical life finds God and communes with Him in one's everyday activities. It connotes total harmony between our faith and our life. But extraordinary mysticism or mysticism of prayer corresponds very much to what earlier authors described as infused contemplation. I personally feel such a division is erroneous and divorces true mysticism from a living process that does not know a dichotomized separation of two types of mysticism. Behind such divisions is a seeming description of mysticism according to the psychic gifts and the gifts of the Holy Spirit that function, rather than a distinction found in Holy Scripture of a growth in viewing the created world in the Logos of God or a more total immersion into the oneness and distinction of the Trinity. According to the Greek Fathers who use this distinction between the Logos mysticism and the trinitarian mysticism, all human beings are called to both stages, since these stages summarize the Gospel call to perfection. It will be this framework that I shall be using in this book, so as an introduction I shall give here a few of the salient features of this concept of mysticism as a growth process to which all are called to enter and share in God's self-communication.

LOGOS MYSTICISM

These mystic-theologians begin from Holy Scripture and develop their own mystical life through asceticism and constant reflection on the revealed word of God. The Trinity, absolute inaccessibility, self-contained in its inner perfection, still seeks, as part of this perfection, of God's essential holiness, to pour itself out in order that its Goodness may be shared. Because we have been created distinct from God, "empty receptacles of God's goodness," in the words of St. Irenaeus,[16] out of God's loving desire to share His life with us, we possess the possibility of growth. And growth means communication interpersonally between God and man through knowledge and love.

God communicates His uncreated energies of love to us through His Word, the *Logos,* through whom He speaks to us and in that Speech we have our being (Jn 1:3; Col 1:16). The abyss between God and nothingness is spanned through the Logos. We find our whole *raison d'être,* reason for being, in and through God's Word. "We are God's work of art, created in Christ Jesus to live the good life as from beginning He had meant us to live it" (Ep 2:10). When God's Logos assumed flesh, our humanity, when He took upon Himself matter, as eternally ordained by God in the total plan of creation, man and the whole material world were irrevocably assumed into that hypostatic union. As divinity and humanity were joined into being "without confusion," as the Council of Chalcedon (451 A.D.) described the hypostatic union, so by analogy man and the world are joined together with divinity without confusion but in a unity of love.

This created world will come into its fullness precisely by entering into a conscious relationship of love with God. Christ is acting within the evolving process of this world to allow the world to be itself and to let man become, through his cooperative creativity, a reconciler with Christ of the whole world (2 Co 5:17-19). Through such a Logos mysticism, the Christian is led progressively into the inner meaning of reality. He is not led away from the created world, but rather he is led into reverence and worship of God as present everywhere within the created world.

We begin the mystical life by entering deeply into the material world and there to find God.[17] The flowers, the trees, birds, animals, the beauties of each new season, the sun, moon, stars, the mountains, lakes, oceans: the whole world reveals to the contemplative the loving presence of God, concerned to give Himself to man in His many gifts. God is contemplated as an almighty Transcendence that is the Source of all created life and is inside of His created world by His uncreated energies of love.[18] The mystic moves ever deeper into reality as he adores the presence of God as the One who "contains" the created world and gives it its "consistency." St. Paul preached to the Athenians this doctrine of the Christian God who " . . . is not far from any of us, since it is in Him that we live and move and exist . . . " (Ac 17:28). Man is not alone; God is everywhere, present and holding up all of existence. This is the vision that Jesus of Nazareth had of His Heavenly Father: "My Father goes on working, and so do I" (Jn 5:17).

The Eastern Fathers developed their doctrine of the participated *logoi,* which they found in the writings of St. Paul and St. John. Each creature possesses a *logos* as its principle of harmony relating it to the Creator. But its "intelligibility" (*logos*) lies hidden beneath its exterior appearances. To penetrate beneath the surface of the phenomena that are perceived by our five senses and to get at this inner *logos* of a given creature would mean, to the early Fathers, to know its place and its role in the whole drama of the history of salvation. It would be to "contemplate" each creature's meaning in the light of Christ's redemption of the entire cosmos. Christ is the greatest reality and He gives meaning to the whole created world.

Man in such a mystical view is God's masterpiece. Uniquely among all creatures, man is privileged by God's gratuitous grace, to be a temple in which the perfect image of the Father, the Divine Logos, dwells. With his intellect and will, by knowing and loving, man is to respond to this living Logos within, and thus God will change this image into the likeness of Himself. Such thinking about man's intimate relationship to Christ remained, for the Eastern Fathers, on the level of a dynamic unfolding of the created *logos* within us, actuated and realized by the love of Jesus Christ and by our personal response to His living presence.

Of all the Greek Fathers, it was chiefly St. Maximus the Confessor (+ 662) who developed a complete vision of a Logos mysticism, summarizing all that Origen, Athanasius, Basil, Gregory of Nazianzus and Gregory of Nyssa had earlier written on this point. For St. Maximus the truly *real* man is he who lives according to his proper *logos* and this logos is modeled on a conscious relationship in loving submission to the Logos living within man that brings forth his potencies to be a loving child of God. We have total being insofar as we have a loving relationship to Christ, allowing Him to fulfill within us that image destined to be brought to perfection in our first creation by the potency God has given us.

This is the beginning of mystical contemplation, what St. Maximus calls *theoria physica,* the contemplation of God in the created world around us. The world is a diaphany through which Jesus Christ is shining, a point Teilhard de Chardin developed from the Greek Fathers. Is such a level of prayer, the beginning stage of mysticism, outside the possibility of the average person? As we learn to turn within ourselves daily in prayer and by means of our passive and active diminishments from daily existence that aid in purifying ourselves of self-centering, we find that Jesus Christ is "present" more readily in our material concerns. We yield our talents to His direction. We seek to live according to God's inner harmony found in each event. We become His servants as we lovingly work to serve others. Thus it is possible for a teacher, a housewife, a business man, a coal miner, a truck driver, a student to possess an inner directing force, a consciousness of Christ's presence within them and they can do all things with full concentration on the given tasks and still remain at least implicitly centered on the presence of Jesus Christ. Besides the moments of deep contemplative prayer, usually in the early morning, such a person in his or her very "profane" work can easily find the presence of Christ and grow in greater adoration and self-surrender to God inside of that situation.

Mother Teresa of Calcutta tells the story of such a

prayerful encounter with Christ in the work of one of her
sisters among the destitute:

> 'During the Mass,' I said, 'you saw that the priest touched
> the Body of Christ with great love and tenderness. When
> you touch the poor today, you too will be touching the
> body of Christ. Give them that same love and tenderness.'
> When they returned several hours later, the new sister
> came up to me, her face shining with joy. 'I have been
> touching the Body of Christ for three hours,' she said. I
> asked her what she had done. 'Just as we arrived, the sister
> brought in a man covered with maggots. He had been
> picked up from a drain. I have been taking care of him, I
> have been touching Christ. I knew it was him,' she said.[19]

This type of mysticism admits of great intensity and
growth in faith, hope and love of God's presence working
through His "two hands," Jesus Christ and the Holy
Spirit, in each event. Our work and our moments of personal prayer both become "places" of discovering God's
loving and active presence. The market place becomes a
point of revealing God in His uncreated energies as we
work with God, according to His "Logos." The division
between the "secular" and the "sacred" worlds breaks
down. Everything becomes sacred to the one contemplating God's Logos in all the material world, in each
on-going event. It is not then in spite of our work that we
strive to become contemplative, but, in doing that very
work in a faith vision, we find ourselves contemplating
God all day long.

TRUE THEOLOGY

As we grow in contemplating the *Logos* within and
outside of ourselves, throughout the entire material

universe, we begin to experience the Logos as relational. He points to the Father and He points from the Father to us. "I am in the Father and the Father in me" (Jn 14:10). Where Christ the Divine Son, is, there also is the Father. "He that sent me is with me and He has not left me alone . . . . The Father abides in me" (Jn 13:29; 14:10). Where the Father and the Son are present, there also is the Holy Spirit, who loves the Father and the Son within us and with us.

Thus we come to the highest level of mysticism in Christianity, the contemplation of the Holy Trinity as dwelling within us and inside the world by the uncreated energies of God's love. The three Persons do not remain inactive within the contemplative. Within, the Father utters His Word; He generates His Son, who is perfectly the Image of the Father, by a perfect response of love which, with the love of the Father for the Son, breathes forth the Holy Spirit.

The Logos not only brings about this trinitarian union with us by His presence, but by His activity within He speaks to us of the Father. The Holy Spirit loves the Father and the Son within us and with us. Christ teaches us to realize His love as Logos for His Father. He teaches us about the Father and the Holy Spirit, but He also associates His activities as Son with our potency to respond likewise in union with Him to a similar act of sonship toward our Heavenly Father. He teaches us how to adore, praise, love, surrender ourselves, dispose of every element that is an obstacle to true Sonship in God by repeating and making effective within us: "Behold, I come to do Thy will." He prays to the Father that we be admitted into the mystery of divine love: "Father, I pray for them also . . . that they may be one in us" (Jn 17:20). He demands of the Father and obtains our participation in His filial surrender of self to the Father: "Father, may the love wherewith you have loved me be in them" (Jn 17:26).

This is the mystical contemplation of the Holy Trinity. In this highest type of mysticism, man progresses farther and farther from earthly thoughts as he becomes gradually assimilated into the very life and love of God. No longer does he speak to God as an object, outside or within himself, but now he knows himself to be caught up into the very life of God through His Son and Holy Spirit. He experiences the unity of the oneness of God. He also experiences his own uniqueness over and against the uniqueness of each Person of the Trinity. This St. Maximus called *theoria theologica,* the essence of true Christian "theology." This is eternal life, "to know you, the only true God, and Jesus Christ whom you have sent" (Jn 17:3).

Here we see how the doctrine of the imageness and likeness of God in every man leads to an ontological union with the Trinity. The principle that guides all theory of contemplation and divinization in the Christian East is that "like can be known only by like." True knowledge of the Trinity that can lead us to true love can be given to us only in the proportion that we are assimilated to the likeness of God through Jesus Christ and His Spirit. Assimilation consists in becoming just and holy as God is. This is salvation in the fullest sense. It is restoration of man to the integrity in which God created him and which He wished him to possess. This is only perfect in the beatific vision, but to those who have attained *theologia* in this life, God reveals Himself no longer through creatures or the *logoi* in creatures, but in His own trinitarian life of active love dwelling within the individual.

This Macarius in his 50 *Spiritual Homilies* calls "pure prayer." It is not judged so much by psychological effects, as the prayer of quiet, ecstasy, transforming union, the espousal and spiritual marriage are so described in the Teresian classification but by the love of God that has permeated us and made us love. St. Symeon the New Theologian (+1022), so-called because he was a mystic who wrote so eloquently about the trinitarian life within the human heart, well describes in one of his hymns the antinomy of the human soul possessing the triune God:

And, as for those who managed to participate in Your
    secrets,
—in an immaterial sensation—to share materially
in your mysteries, formidable and for all unspeakable . . .
they are the ones who have received pure contemplation,
from the One who was in the beginning, before all creation,
begotten of the Father, and with the Spirit, Son, God and
    Word,
triple light in unity but unique light in the three.
Two aspects of a unique light: Father, Son and Spirit,
for it is indivisible in the three Persons, without confusion,
these three Persons in whom, according to the
divine nature, there is but one power,
one glory, one authority and one will.
All three appear to me in one unique face,
like two beautiful eyes filled with light.
How will the eye see without the face, tell me?
But without eyes it is useless to speak of the face,
deprived as it is of the essential, or better still of every-
    thing![20]

This life in the Trinity knows no static moment of having arrived at a peak with no more illumination and divine love to receive from the indwelling presence of the Trinity. "The beginning of his race is his end and the end is the beginning. Perfection has no end, there again the beginning is the end."[21]

One who sees this Divine Light cannot be satisfied; yet there is peace and joy. Such a mystic sees the triune God alone, looks for nothing else. He sees nothing of the visible or intellectual things around him except as these are in the Trinity that he alone sees. Everything has its being in that Trinity, in that Light. Yet having seen the Trinity by a deepening and intense faith, hope and love, such a mystic lives on a deeper plane, ever in contact with immaterial realities inside of the material creation that surrounds him. Now he looks at the sense objects in this world and sees only God at their heart. Wealth, the beauties of nature, intelligent persons, works of art, music, beautiful women, smiling babies, all lead him to see God and to know His divine mind by giving him knowledge how to praise God in all of His manifestations of love in creatures given as gifts to man. Such a mystic "intuits" the oneness of God's energetic love and its threeness in inter-relationships that he himself experiences as he lives inside of the very trinitarian relationships and shares in their relatedness.

There is no other way of truly knowing God and hence fully loving Him except that God touch the individual with His light so that he sees as did Jesus in His humanity. When God touches man with His light, he then knows that God knows and loves him. Who sees God knows that God sees Him. And he knows that he knows God. This knowledge turns into divine love, *agape,* which is now no thing but is the very essence of God touching man and giving Himself in that loving relationship.

This light of God is a gradual revelation of God's

presence within man and without. The mystic understands that, although God is immovable, yet He is always in movement. He fills all things, transcends all. He is immaterial, yet He pervades all matter. He has no mouth to speak, yet He speaks His Word within man. He has no hand to grasp man and guide him but man knows God touches him with His divine hand and raises him up to gaze on His face. That hand gives an assurance, a power and a certainty that nothing can take away. Gradually the presence of the indwelling Trinity is seen as a light that is a "form that is formless," dwelling constantly within man.

THE TRINITY AS LIGHT

The indwelling presence of the Trinity as light within man permeates his whole being and integrates the body, soul and spirit levels into a "whole" human being, consumed by love for God. One sees His light everywhere, adores Him in great humility, surrenders himself in total service. He is instructed by God in the things of God. Above all, he knows at each moment what is the will of God for him. This is why true mysticism and the ultimate stages of it bring us to true Christian perfection. "This is the only way to discover the will of God and know what is good, what it is that God wants, what is the perfect thing to do" (Rm 12:2).

It is this that God calls all of us to receive. He has created us to enter into His most intimate communication of Himself to us through Jesus Christ in His Holy Spirit. We are destined by God to progress into a greater transformation, as a seed into a flowering tree, through the knowledge and contemplative experience of knowing God and of being known and loved by Him. This knowledge

and love God wished to give to all of His children when He
called them "to be holy and spotless, and to live through
love in his presence" (Ep 1:4).

The words of St. Symeon form a fitting close to this
chapter:

> . . . you have put on Christ consciously
>   and knowingly
> who radiates, is resplendent in the glory
>   of the divinity
> and who in a light most clear completely
>   transforms you,
> leaving you in a way unchanged yet in a way you are
>   now two things,
> both one and the other: god by adoption and completely
>   man by nature.
> So, then come and place yourself with us,
>   O my brother,
> on the mountain of divine knowledge
>   of divine contemplation
> and together let us hear the Father's voice.[21]

2

The Mystery of the Trinity

There burns within the heart of modern man a desire to "experience" God. Like Moses, he too has tried to approach the "Burning Bush" by his own power. He has sought to touch and handle the *Absolute* by means of his own images and ideas. Yet God, "a consuming fire" (Heb 12:29), defies such cardboard constructions in His beyondness and unpossessableness.

No doubt the impersonalism of our technological world drives us toward a personalism that roots our identity in more than "things" that perish. Still technology has created the means, such as computer science, that give us instant communication with all parts of our universe. Distances and time shrink through satellite communication so that we can be psychologically "present" to persons and events instantaneously throughout the whole world. The problems of Africans and Chinese become our problems as we "see" them as real persons and no longer as vague, faraway nations.

But the greatest surge towards personalism comes through the very de-fault of religions themselves to present a God that is intimately present to us, concerned and involved in our everyday lives. And even when preachers speak about God in personalistic terms as "He" or the Father, Son and Holy Spirit, all too often the three Persons of the Trinity are presented as three "objects" to whom we can address all of our needs.

EXPERIENCE THE TRINITY

Even when Christians give verbal acknowledgment to the truth of the Trinity, as Karl Rahner says, the majority of Christians remain "monotheists," that is, they pray to a God who is "outside" or "up there."

> . . . despite their orthodox confession of the Trinity, Christians are, in their practical life, almost mere "monotheists." We must be willing to admit that, should the doctrine of the Trinity have to be dropped as false, the major part of religious literature could well remain virtually unchanged . . . Nowadays when we speak of God's incarnation, the theological and religious emphasis lies only on the fact that "God" became man, that "one" of the divine persons (of the Trinity) took on the flesh, and not on the fact that this person is precisely the person of the Logos.[1]

R. Panikkar divides spirituality into three types that have been with human beings as long as they have practised any form of religion.[2] The lowest level of man relating to God is *iconolatry.* Man builds for himself an *icon,* an image, an idol of God that he adores as though his projections were really true. Such a God is easily handled by man through his prayers, rituals and concepts about God.

The second type of spirituality deals with God as a person or, as in Christianity, three persons in one God.

This is a higher level of human consciousness where God takes on a personality. He loves, judges, pardons, punishes and rewards. He does everything we as persons do without, however, our human imperfections. There is devotion and loving obedience to God through a person-to-person dialogue. But in the very communication between God and ourselves, is there not also a danger that we project our desires into the person of God so that we end up creating Him according to our own image?

The third level of spirituality has such an exalted idea of God that the very idea itself must be transcended. Dialogue between persons, God and ourselves, yields to *mystery.* In an *apophatic* experience God and man are experienced as an immanent union of two in one where duality yields to *advaita,* the Hindu word for non-duality.

In such a level of Christian spirituality the *oneness* of God and His *threeness* are experienced, not through objectivization, but through mystery. In God's continuous process of communicating Himself to us, we are to open ourselves to His self-communication as *absolute truth* and as *absolute love*[3] within the context of God's salvific history.

A REVEALED MYSTERY

The mystery of the Trinity has been revealed to us in Holy Scripture. Revelation is a communication, a manifestation of truths by God who makes them known to us. God positively intervenes to disclose to human beings truths by means of signs. And so we can know much about God through His revelation in His created, material world. He reveals more of Himself as a living Person to His Chosen People through the Law and the Prophets.

But it is when His Word becomes incarnate that God most fully reveals Himself, no longer in words and signs, but in the one Word and Sacrament, Jesus Christ. We have no way of knowing the Father but through seeing Him in His Son (Jn 14:9). We have no way of receiving God's love for us except through receiving the personalized love of Jesus Christ. "As the Father loves me, so I love you" (Jn 15:9).

If God is love by essence, then He is always seeking by His nature to share His being by communicating His presence. In the Christian religion God becomes a God-toward-others by communicating Himself through His Word in His Spirit of love. God creates the whole world as good, as a sign of His burning desire to give Himself in faithful communication through His Word. The world at its interior is filled with the self-communicating Trinity. God is filling the universe with His loving Self. His un-created energies swirl through and fill all creatures with His loving, creative presence (Ps 33:4-9). God delights to give Himself through His Word to His creatures.

> . . . I was by his side, a master craftsman,
> delighting him day after day,
> ever at play in his presence,
> at play everywhere in his world,
> delighting to be with the sons of men (Pr 8:29-31).

Everything flows out of God's exuberant fullness of being and *becomes* a reality in His communicating Word. He speaks through His Word and oceans and mountains, birds and beasts, flowers and all living things spring into being under His laughing, joyful gaze. Nothing that is can escape His loving touch, His presence as Giver of life. Not only does God communicate Himself in creation, but He is a sustaining, directing God. He evolves His presence that is locked into His creation through His Word that is continually being communicated over millions of years.

But in God's Word made flesh we have been privileged to receive the fullness of His communicating glory and life itself.

> The Word was made flesh,
> He lived among us,
> and we saw his glory,
> the glory that is his as the only Son of the Father,
> full of grace and truth (Jn 1:14).

God's fullest revelation is made in His incarnate Word, Jesus Christ. For in Him we have not only words, but we have the one Word that is the perfect copy of God's nature. In Him we can come not only to know God's very nature but we can be brought into a loving communion with God's being. We can become truly participators of God's very own nature (2 P 1:4). The author of *Letter to the Hebrews* describes this revelation in God's incarnate Word:

> At various times in the past and in various different ways, God spoke to our ancestors through the prophets; but in our own time, the last days, he has spoken to us through his Son, the Son that he has appointed to inherit everything and through whom he made everything there is. He is the radiant light of God's glory and the perfect copy of his nature, sustaining the universe by his powerful command; and now that he has destroyed the defilement of sin, he has gone to take his place in heaven at the right hand of divine Majesty. So he is now as far above the angels as the title

which he has inherited is higher than their own name (Heb 1:1-4).

Knowing the Word Incarnate, we can now know the Father and His Spirit in whom the Word makes known to us the Father. We, by listening to the Word enfleshed for love of us, can know what the inner life of the Trinity is like. It is through the Word made flesh that we can learn of the communitarian sharing within the Trinity, model of the same trinitarian energies of love that are shared with us human beings *ad extra,* outside of that "essential" life of the triune God. We can be caught up in the absolute reality that is at the heart of all other reality, that which is the beginning and the end of all being.

God the Father, the "unoriginated Source of being," in absolute silence, in a communication of love impossible for human beings to understand, speaks His one eternal Word through His Spirit of Love. In that one Word, the Father is perfectly present, totally self-giving to His Son. "In him lives the fullness of divinity" (Col 2:9).

In His Spirit, the Father also hears His Word come back to Him in a perfect, eternal "yes" of total surrendering Love that is again the Holy Spirit. The Trinity is a reciprocal community of a movement of the Spirit of Love between Father and Son. Our weak minds cannot fathom the peace and joy, the ardent excitement and exuberant self-surrender that flow in a reposeful motion between Father and Son through the Holy Spirit. God becomes real only because He can communicate in Love with His Word. His Word gives Him His identity as Father. But that means eternal self-giving to the Other, His Word in Love.

Such an entrance into the very nature of God and His trinitarian community of three relational Persons on the part of us human beings is impossible outside of God's revelation. The doctrine of the Trinity and God's one nature is a truth impossible to be grasped by our natural cognition. M.J. Scheeben writes:

> Without belief in God's revelation it cannot be known at all; and even for believers it is incomprehensible in an exceptionally high degree, indeed, in the highest degree. There it is a mystery in the truest, highest, most beautiful sense of the word.[4]

Jesus Christ, however, bridges the abyss of our inability ever to come to know and experience God as He is in truth and love. There can be no true knowledge of God except through Jesus Christ. "Everything has been entrusted to me by my Father; and no one knows the Son except the Father, just as no one knows the Father except the Son and those to whom the Son chooses to reveal him" (Mt 11:27). Jesus speaks the words of God (Jn 4:34). He speaks what the Father has taught Him (Jn 8:28). His words are "spirit and life" (Jn 6:63). Jesus in His humanity is life because He lives by the living Father (Jn 6:58). He is also light and we are light in Him (Ep 5:8) because He comes from the light that is the Father. "Light from Light, true God from true God," as the Nicene-Constantinople creed expresses it.

What is there interior to Christ leads us into the interior of God Himself. He and only He could have become incarnate since He by His nature is the Word of God. He proceeds eternally from the Father in the likeness of nature. The Son has everything that He possesses from the Father. He is the expressed Image of the Father and so He can bring perfectly to us that likeness of the Father. He is the Word that issues forth from the Mind of God. Hence the Word is most suited within the Trinity to become the expressed self-realization of the Godhead.[5]

The Father, being the unoriginated source of all being, is in a way no being. How could no-being become incarnate and become a being? In a way the Father has all His meaning in His Son. He, the Father, can never stand alone as a self-existing being or person. What is true within the Trinity is true of God's missions in relationship to the human race. The Word perfectly leads us to the Father and makes it possible for us to become His children and brothers and sisters of Jesus Christ in His Spirit. In this history of salvation the Father through His Word incarnate, just as the trinitarian Father, has His personhood in His Son.

The Spirit could not become the incarnate Word that would speak to us about the Father even though He proceeds from the Source, the Father. The Spirit is the binding love between the Father and the Son. The same Spirit is the binding love between us united to Jesus and the Father. The Spirit could not have been the means to reveal the Father to us since He has His whole being from the Father through the Son. Only the Son reflects the Father's full personhood and therefore He alone can be the image of the Father to us in the Incarnation. It is the Spirit who reveals to us not the Father but the mutual love of the Father and the Son and this especially when Jesus Christ has died on the Cross. M. Scheeben well describes this:

In the Godhead the mutual love of the Son and the Father pours itself out in the production of the Holy Spirit, who issues from their common heart, in whom both surrender their heart's blood, and to whom they give themselves as

the pledge of their infinite love. In order worthily to represent this infinitely perfect surrender to His Father, the
Logos wished in His humanity to pour forth His blood
from His heart to the last drop, that blood in which and
through which the Holy Spirit gave life to His Humanity,
the blood that was pervaded, sanctified, and scented with
heavenly loveliness, and so ascended to God with such
pleasing fragrance. . . . He (the Spirit) urges on the God-
man to His sacrifice, and brings the oblation itself into the
presence of the Father, uniting it to the eternal homage of
love, which is He Himself.[6]

THE DIVINE ECONOMY

We can see, therefore, that the ineffable mystery of
the Trinity, that escapes our own human comprehension,
can, however, be known and experienced in and through
Jesus Christ and the Holy Spirit. God not only deemed to
reveal the truth of this mystery to us but in that revelation
He has made the mystery of the Trinity the beginning and
the end of all reality. God effects our fulfillment precisely
in and through the activities of the triune God in the context of our history of salvation.

We come not only to know but also to experience the
triune God within what Rahner calls the biblical data
about the "economic" Trinity. "Economia" (*oikonomia*
in Greek) etymologically refers to the well running of a
household. In theology it usually refers to any divine activity in relationship to creatures. Thus theologians speak
of "the economy of salvation." Among the Greek Fathers
theology properly so-called concerns itself with teaching
about the Divine Being itself, namely, the Holy Trinity.
The exterior manifestations of God, the Holy Trinity
known in its relation to created being, belong to the realm
of economy.[7]

It is such a meaning, namely, the relationships of the Trinity toward the created world, especially toward human beings, that Karl Rahner states very emphatically in his principle: "The 'economic Trinity' is the 'immanent Trinity' and the 'immanent Trinity' is the 'economic' Trinity."[8] Such a thesis is solidly rooted also in the Greek patristic theologizing about the mystery of the Trinity in relationship to us. There must be a connection between the Trinity and ourselves. In identifying the Trinity of the economy of salvation with the immanent Trinity (the life within the very Trinity of the Father, Son and Holy Spirit, without any reference to the created order) Rahner, along with the Greek Fathers as well as M. Scheeben, seeks to stress the personalism of the three Divine Persons in their one "essential" act of self-communication to human beings. If this were not so, Rahner argues, "God would be the "giver," not the *gift itself,* he would "give himself" only to the extent that he communicates a gift distinct from himself."[9]

What hinges very strongly and importantly upon this thesis of the similarity between the immanent, trinitarian "activities" and the economic "activities" is the question whether we human beings are so loved by God that we are radically transformed by God's gift of Himself and by His very own transforming Persons, the Son and the Holy Spirit, or whether we are merely extrinsically "affiliated" with God in a salvation of decree and not of true "regeneration."

GOD'S ESSENCE AND ENERGIES

Among the early Greek Fathers, such as Sts. Basil, Gregory of Nazianzus and Gregory of Nyssa, who were most responsible for articulating a theology of the Trinity, and for St. Gregory Palamas of the 14th century, the problem of whether man could actually "experience" God directly and immediately was seen as crucial to the foundational truths of Christianity. Scripture revealed that God was love, in constant communication and self-giving to mankind. Jesus Christ came to give us the life of God, that we might have it more abundantly (Jn 10:10). Eternal life was to be a knowing experience, a receiving of God the Father and Son as Gift. "And eternal life is this: to know you, the only true God, and Jesus Christ whom you have sent" (Jn 17:3). St. Paul insists that we are made to be sons of God, children of God (Rm 8:15; Ga 4:6). Jesus insisted that man must be born from above, of the Spirit (Jn 3:3-5). He and His Father would come and abide within those Christians who obey His commandments (Jn 14:23). All of us were called to be divinized as children of God and participators of His very own nature (2 P 1:4).

But how can we experience God whom, Scripture says also, no man has ever been able to see? Scripture clearly teaches us that we can never come to know God perfectly. In this earthly existence we shall never see Him face to face. But God does show Himself to us as He did to Moses, but it is only His "back" that we see. "Then I will take my hand away and you shall see the back of me; but my face is not to be seen" (Ex 33:23). We can never see Him fully. "No one has ever seen God" (1 Jn 4:12; Jn 1:18; 6:46). We would have to be God in order to receive the fullness of God as gift. To know Him fully we would have to share in His very own nature. In spite, therefore, of the revelation of the Father's love made to us by His Son, Jesus Christ, we shall never know Him fully. No matter how burning is the fire in the heart of the mystic for

greater union with God, there will always be something un-
fathomable about God.

Jesus Christ through His Holy Spirit makes it possible
that we can "know" and experience God as our loving
Father. As we become healed by the infinite love of Jesus
poured out on the cross, while He still lives within us, we
begin to live more constantly in the communication of
God's love for us in each moment. We enter into a state of
always becoming more and more God's loving children.
Less and less does God become an outside object to which
we speak our prayers in order that we can change Him. We
go to prayer now, not any longer to change God's attitude
toward us, but rather to be changed by Him into His loving
children.

We live now in "mystery" through an increase of
faith, hope and love that God, Father, Son and Spirit, are
to be found inside of each event as uncreated energies of
love.

ENERGIES OF LOVE

The doctrine of the Greek Fathers concerning grace
primarily as God as uncreated energies of love has much to
teach us. If we are to live in the mystery of God's love in
each moment, then we must find Him essentially as one
God, loving us with an everlasting, unchanging love. But if
this love is to transform us into loving persons who can live
in the mystery of oneness and uniqueness toward all
human beings that we meet, then these loving energies
must also bring us into the personal and unique love activities of the three Persons.

God's love will too easily be objectivized as a thing
with which He loves us unless the Father is now experi-

enced by us as begetting us into new life in His only begotten Son. The love of Jesus Christ will be lost in His past deeds, especially His death on the cross, unless we can *now* in this present moment experience His outpoured love for each of us individually as we are caught up in the current of His total surrender of Himself to return the Father's love in His Holy Spirit.

The Holy Spirit will all too easily be relegated to a Divine Person who gives us gifts so that we may function properly. We must *now* experience the mystery of how the Spirit is being breathed into our hearts by the Father through His Son.

The early Fathers lived daily in the mystery of the Triune God through experiencing God as energies of love. They knew that they could never know or experience the essence of God which always remained unknowable and incomprehensible to created man. This Karl Rahner calls the "immanent" Trinity. But they knew from Holy Scripture, especially through the work of Jesus Christ and His Holy Spirit, that God does communicate Himself to man in a new knowing and a new participation through His energies. These energies are God's mode of existing in relationship to His created world, especially to man. These energies are not *things,* as an extrinsic "grace" that God heaps upon us, but they are truly God Himself as *Gift.*

Roland Zimany accurately describes the distinction between God's essence and His energies:

> God, the essential Trinity, is the Giver, and God in His energies, which enable God to be known outside Himself and which are inseparable from the divine nature which they manifest, is the gift of uncreated grace.[10]

DIVINIZATION

With the divine energies always surrounding us and
lovingly calling us to respond to God's Word living within
us and within the context of our existential life, we reach
our highest development in the continued cooperation
(*synergy*) with God's energetic presence. When we continuously cooperate with God's grace His divine,
uncreated energies manifested to us in the context of our
daily lives, we enter into the process of *theosis* or divinization which is the total integration of the body-soul-spirit
relationships of man with God. This is the end of God's
creation of man as His masterpiece, endowed with an
orientation to grow daily into the image and likeness of
God that is Jesus Christ.

This divinization process unites us with God in His
energies through a union by grace. We are made participators in the divine nature, without, however, changing
our human nature into the divine. We are in communication with the full triune God, yet God remains *essentially*
unknowable to us. According to the Eastern Fathers, God's
energies of love have a holistic influence of divinizing the
whole person, body, soul and spirit. And as we are divinized into the likeness of Jesus Christ, God effects through
our cooperation to "spiritualize" the entire cosmos, bringing it into the resurrectional influence of Jesus Christ who
is bringing all things into fullness (Col 1:20).

For St. Gregory Palamas, who summarizes in his 14th
century writings the common doctrine of the earlier Greek
Fathers on the distinction between God's essence and His
uncreated energies, every "essence" has to have an
"energy" if it is to be more than merely "possible." God is

the most real of all realities. He has real existence in the world insofar as He is manifested to the world. We could also say that He is essentially love only if He communicates Himself as love to others. This is why Rahner can insist that the "immanent" Trinity is also the "economic" Trinity. God has real existence in the world insofar as He creates the world, i.e., gives it existence by giving it a share in His own real existence in and through the energies. But He has greater "presence" to this world when He gives Himself in a personal way by giving us His Son and His Spirit and through them He shares His very own life by divinizing us into His very own children. His energies of love transform us, if we cooperate, into a oneness with His only begotten Son, Jesus Christ, and yet in that oneness we find our uniqueness to which God calls us when He calls us by our very own name." "I have called you by your name, you are mine" (Is 43:1).

The patristic teaching of the energies as distinct from God's essence is the basis of all mystical experience. We can truly come to know and love God and we can be known and loved by God. The doctrine of the Trinity becomes now a living experience of the one and united God, essentially love, and always the same in His relationship to us but now manifested to us in His energies meeting us at each moment. We enter into deep and tender interpersonal relationships with each Divine Person, Father, Son and Holy Spirit since their relationships within the "immanent" Trinity are the basis also for their relationships in their energies as the "economic" Trinity continually touches us. A unique Father loves us uniquely in the unique personality of His only begotten Son through the unique loving relationship of the Spirit that binds Father, Son and ourselves into a oneness and yet into an on-going discovery in mystery of all of our uniqueness as persons, capable of surrendering ourselves in love to each other.[11]

This is our human dignity: to be called children of God and we really are such by the uncreated energies of God as they touch us at each moment and call us into a more intimate divinization as His children.

> Think of the love that the Father has lavished on us,
> by letting us be called God's children;
> and that is what we are . . .
> My dear people, we are already the children of God
> but what we are to be in the future has not yet been revealed;
> all we know is, that when it is revealed
> we shall be like him
> because we shall see him as he really is (1 Jn 3:1-2).

Such an on-going process is in the order of non-conceptualization. It must be experienced by the Spirit of Jesus Christ. And to those who approach the triune God as energies loving them into new being at each moment of their lives, in brokenness and conversion of their lives in total gift back to God, a superior knowledge will be given. It will be in mystery that they will comprehend the incomprehensible God.

AN APOPHATIC THEOLOGY

Before we can approach the indwelling Trinity of Father, Son and Holy Spirit begetting us through their unique, personal relationships to us in their energies of love, one last thing, which summarizes what has been the main thrust of this chapter, needs to be developed. This is to point out the apophatic approach to the Divine Trinity which corrective alone prevents us from objectivizing God or the three Persons into three Gods. It is only in such a humble recognition of our inability to possess God by our own human power that God in His faithfulness to His *Hesed* Covenant does come down to our littleness and raises us up to a new level of being in His love.

The highest union, the infused union of the Trinity, in which God communicates Himself directly to us through His Word in His Spirit, is not achieved in any conceptual knowledge but in an immediate, experiential knowledge wherein He opens Himself to us. We can never come to this knowledge through any concept, any rationalization or any discursive method of our own. God, purely and simply in His Transcendence, reveals Himself to us when He wishes. After years of our own preparation and cooperation through continued purification, God sees that we are humble enough to be so open to Him as to see Him in everything and to see ourselves as an off-shoot of God's overflowing love.

Thus a unique charcteristic of the Eastern Fathers is their emphasis on this highest type of contemplation of the Trinity in terms of an apophatic theology. *Apophatic* is usually translated as negative, but this is to misunderstand the nuanced mysticism of these early Fathers. The accent is entirely on God doing the revealing, giving the Gift of Himself; no longer is the emphasis on ourselves and our personal activities. God, who is so infinitely perfect and good, the incomprehensible, deigns to allow us to know Him in some fashion or other by way of a direct experience.

The best description of this approach is given by Vladimir Lossky:

The negative way of the knowledge of God is an ascendant undertaking of the mind that progressively eliminates all positive attributes of the object it wishes to attain, in order to culminate finally in a kind of apprehension by supreme ignorance of Him who cannot be an object of knowledge. We can say that it is an intellectual experience of the mind's failure when confronted with something beyond the conceivable. In fact, consciousness of the failure of human understanding constitutes an element common to all that we can call *apophasis,* or negative theology, whether this apophasis remains within the limits of intellection, simply declaring the radical lack of correspondence between our mind and the reality it wishes to attain, or whether it wishes to surpass the limits of understanding, imparting to the ignorance of what God is in His inaccessible nature the value of a mystical knowledge superior to the intellect.[12]

The positive theology (*cataphatic*), as also in our positive, discursive prayer-life, uses the perfections that we find in creatures about us, and from this limited knowledge, we are able to know something about the infinite perfections of God. We have pointed out the confining spirit of such a level of objectivizing God, usually according to our desires, even when we have reached a high level of person-to-person relationship. We must move from a beginning stage of positive concept of God to a higher stage. It is a paradox that in utter darkness God reveals Himself. We remove ourselves progressively more and more from any possibility of coming to know God by our own power, and in that utter state of humility and nothingness and abasement before God, we witness to that ontological truth that we are creatures totally dependent on God. He then comes down and shows Himself to us in that darkness or incapacity of our own natural faculties. It is climbing the heights of God's presence where presence and transcendence are the same thing. And in that presence we become immanently present to Him in a union of knowledge and love that only God, the Giver, can give us with Himself as the Gift.

With Moses we have to climb up the mountain to reach God by a knowing that is unknowing, a darkness that is luminous. As we separate ourselves from all limitations we place on God and from all attachments to our own self-love, we reach the top of the mountain. There in the darkness of the storming clouds we hear the notes of the trumpet and we see those lights that no human method could ever give us. Ultimately no human mind, no teacher, no technique could ever bring us God's personalized Gift of Himself. God has to take over and communicate Himself directly. No one but God can give us this experience.

St. John Damascene describes the apophatic approach that avoids any placing of God into a class of being like other existing things:

> God is infinite and incomprehensible and all that is comprehensible about Him is His infinity and incomprehensibility. All that we can say cataphatically concerning God does not show forth His nature, but things that relate to His nature. God does not belong to a class of existing things. He receives no existence, but is above all existing things. If all forms of knowledge have to do with what exists, that which is above knowledge must be above all (created) essence, and what is above essence must be above knowledge.[13]

Thus, with the apophatic approach as background, in

prayerful humility and a sense of our deep unworthiness to approach God to probe into the *how* He communicates Himself to us, we can turn to that union to which God calls us. It is a path that leads us beyond idols and images, even beyond our objectivizing God as a Person to whom we can address ourselves as to another created being. It is a knowledge of experience that admits of an infinite growth because this knowledge surpasses all human understanding and becomes identified with true love. To know the Trinity in this sense of mystery is to love God through the Spirit of Jesus Christ as God loves us.

The Godhead and Father

One of the great classics in Byzantine iconography is the icon of the *Trinity,* painted by the Russian monk, Andrei Rublev (c. 1408-1425). He used an ancient, traditional image, known in the East from the earliest centuries,[1] of the apparition of the three angels to Abraham by the oak of Mambre (Gn 18) to describe in iconic form the dogmatic teaching of the one Godhead and the three Persons in the Trinity. Using a circle as the basic form of composition, and intersecting circles and very vivid colors: blue, green, pink, brown, and purple, the iconographer depicts the three Persons: Father, Son, and Holy Spirit as three angels brought into a oneness of deep peace and joyfulness.[2]

Unlike so many attempts in Western art to depict the Trinity in images of a grey-bearded Father, with a more youthful Son holding the globe of the world and the Spirit as a dove hovering over both of them,[3] this Byzantine statement avoids the "objectivization" of making the Divine Persons look like human ones. It is a mystical vision, through harmony and relationship of colors and circular lines, of the inner trinitarian life of movement and rest, peace and joy, of a community of three in a oneness that constantly feeds to the Godhead for it is a nameless form

which constantly feeds back through its circular movement
from one person to the other two. It captures the meaning
in the words of Pseudo-Dionysius:

> Circular movement signifies that God remains identical
> with Himself, that He envelops in synthesis the in-
> termediate parts and the extremities, which are at the same
> time containers and contained, and that He recalls to
> Himself all that has gone forth from Him.[4]

In this icon, depicted on the cover of this book, we see
the Father as the angel on the left, as a figure subdued and
retiring, suggesting the apophatic belief in the
unknowability directly of the Father or Godhead of the
Trinity except through the Son who is the angelic figure in
the center. He dominates the entire icon as He gazes lovingly at the Father, while pointing his two fingers, sym-
bolical of His two natures, divine and human, toward the
Eucharistic chalice on the white table before them, in
which there is the head of a sacrificial animal. The Holy
Spirit is seen as the third angel on the right, dressed in a
green cloak, the sign of youth and fullness of powers.

We are caught up into the circular movement and
brought into the very life of the triune God where there is
distinction of Persons, yet oneness of nature. We seem to
capture part of the paradox of the inner trinitarian life: the
Godhead is complete rest and self-repose, freed of all activity. Yet the three Persons possess an active dimension as
they gaze at each other and seem to move eternally from
one to the other in a stillness that hints at a loving communication in the power of silence.

It is an "unmoving movement" that suggests the

words of Meister Eckhart, the 14th century Rhenish, Dominican mystic:

> What is this play? It is His eternal Son. There has always been this play going on in the Father-nature. Play and audience are the same. The Father's view of His own nature is His Son. The Father embraces His own nature in the quiet darkness of His eternal essence which is known to none except Himself. The *glance* returned by His own nature is His eternal Son. So the Son embraces the Father in His nature, for He is the same as His Father, in His nature. Thus, from the Father's embrace of His own nature there comes this eternal playing of the Son. This play was played eternally before all creatures . . . the Son has eternally been playing before the Father as the Father has before His Son. The playing (as an act) of the two is the Holy Spirit in whom they both disport themselves and He disports Himself in (them) both. Sport and players are the same. Their nature (is) proceeding in itself. 'God is a fountain flowing into itself,' as St. Dionysius says.[5]

FROM PERSONS TO NATURE

Father Th. de Regnon, S.J., in his classical work on the Holy Trinity, shows the difference between the Western and the Eastern approaches to the doctrine of the Trinity:

> Latin philosophy first considers the nature in itself and proceeds to the agent; Greek philosophy first considers the agent and afterwards passes through it to find the nature. The Latins think of personality as a mode of nature; the Greeks think of nature as the content of the person.[6]

V. Lossky points out that both approaches are valid, provided the Latin approach does not attribute to the divine essence a supremacy over the three persons, nor the second (that of the Eastern approach) to the three persons a supremacy over the common nature.[7] There is value in the Eastern approach that is rooted in Holy Scripture with its accent on the incomprehensible nature of the Godhead. Yet God does communicate Himself to us in the triune, personal relationships. It is a mystical approach, like Rublev's icon, that *retains mystery* and experience.

THE GODHEAD AS SOURCE

The Greek Fathers begin with the Godhead, not as the total essence of God, made up of three Persons, but rather as the "unoriginated Source," the principal root of unity in the Trinity. This is seen as the Father and not so much abstractly as the "essence" of God. St. Gregory of Nazianzus, the great 4th century Greek theologian who wrote so eloquently about the Trinity, describes the Father as the source and goal of diversity or personal relationships within the Trinity.

> The nature is one in three; it is God; but that which makes the unity is the Father, from whom and to whom the order of persons runs its course, not in such a way that the nature is confused, but that it is possessed without distinction of time or of will or of power.[8]

This is Yahweh, God of Israel who revealed to Moses his darkness: "For man cannot see me and live" (Ex 33:20). The six-winged seraphs chanted before His heavenly throne: "Holy, holy, holy is Yahweh Sabaoth. His glory fills the whole earth" (Is 6:3). He is the "unmanifested" or "undifferentiated" dimension of God's nature, in the words of Pseudo-Dionysius.[9] No name can be truly given the Ultimate Ground out of which all other being comes. It is the Absolute Beginning, the Immovable Rest from which all movement and differentiation in being come.

This Godhead is the "unnatured nature" in Meister Eckhart's phrase. Eckhart, along with many of the great mystics of all religions, calls this Godhead the *Abyss,* the Desert, the wilderness, prior to movement, even of the personalistic dynamism of the Trinity. One cannot call this Absolute a being for it is beyond all being. It does not receive *existence* to become a be-ing but it is the underived Origin of all being.

And even though Jesus reveals this Godhead as our Father and His Father, as Godhead, it cannot say Father which term implies a being of such and such a relationship. R. Panikkar links this with the Buddhist apophaticism of the Void.

> Is it not here, truly speaking, in this essential apophatism of the 'person' of the Father, is this *kenosis* of Being at its very source, that the buddhist experience of *nirvana* and *synyata* (emptiness) should be situated? One is led onwards towards the 'absolute goal' and at the end one finds nothing, because there is nothing, not even Being. 'God created out of nothing' (ex nihilo), certainly, i.e. out of himself (a Deo)—a buddhist will say.[10]

This Godhead is "motionless unity and balanced Stillness and is the Source of all emanations."[11] As Godhead, no Word is yet spoken to relate itself to as Mind. In the Godhead is the fullness of being, the Silence out of which will come relational communication. God as Stillness is the Godhead waiting to move from Silence to

Speech, from perfect repose and motionlessness to sharing love in movement towards Another.

Thomas Merton, evidently relying on Buddhist literature and the writings of Meister Eckhart, describes well the Godhead as desert and the Void:

> The uncreated is waste and emptiness to the creature. Not even sand. Not even stone. Not even darkness and night. A burning wilderness would at least be "something." It burns and is wild. But the Uncreated is no something. Waste. Emptiness. Total poverty of the Creator; yet from this poverty springs everything. The waste is inexhaustible. Infinite Zero. Everything wants to return to it and cannot. For who can return "nowhere"? But for each of us there is a point of nowhereness in the middle of movement, a point of nothingness in the midst of being: the incomparable point not to be discovered by insight. If you seek it you do not find it. If you stop seeking, it is there. But you must not turn to it. Once you become aware of yourself as seeker, you are lost. But if you are content to be lost you will be found without knowing it, precisely because you are lost, for you are, at last, nowhere.[12]

This "Infinite Zero" does not imply sheer negativity. Because of the Godhead's fullness of richness, it cannot be classified in quantified numbers or in categories of beings that have an origin of their being. The Godhead is beyond all being and yet is found in all being, including ourselves. Deeply permeating our whole being and yet beyond even our own consciousness of what constitutes our proper "being" is this Source and Origin. Divinity lies imbedded in our "innermost self" that Dr. Carl Rogers describes as the innermost core of our nature.[13]

This center of our being, that plunges beyond our preconditioning, past experiences, is a formless chaos out of which new life is to come. It meets the formless Void of the Godhead and it is here that we most belong in a oneness to God. This spark of divinity, the "fünklein" of Eckhart, is in all things and yet God has not yet breathed His hovering Spirit over this chaos to bring forth being. The Godhead tremulously holds us and the whole world in His grasp that escapes all names.

Nietzsche once wrote: "One must possess a chaos within to give birth to a star."[14] It is here that all true contemplation leads: to a knowing beyond our knowing. In silence we come into the Void. We merge with the darkness of the Godhead. No longer is God an "object" toward which we go in prayer to communicate and to receive some "things." He truly becomes the illimitable Ocean of all being.

Rudolf Otto expresses such a mysticism:

> He (the mystic) has got rid of the conceived and apprehended God, because God has now become his inward power, by which he lives, but upon which he reflects less, the more completely and powerfully he lives in the Divine.[15]

The Ocean covers everything and does not need to become wet since all things are wet because of its complete covering of everything.

THE TRINITY

Out of the Void God stirs as personal Source, the Father, to want to share His fullness of being. The dark side of God's *no-thingness* turns to light as God wishes to know Himself by actuating His ocean of unlimited, infinite being into Meaningfulness. The Godhead would remain forever the Void if it were not revealed and known through the Trinity. The Father is the Godhead as Mystery, coming forth and seeking understanding. The Father moves the Godhead from pure repose to meaningful, loving motion as He pours the fullness of His divinity into His Son (Col 2:9).

Now God has a name, Father, because His meaningfulness is expressed in His self-giving to His Son, through His Spirit of Love. God would always have remained the Void had it not been through the revelation of Christianity that God is a Father precisely through His only begotten Son and His Spirit. The trinitarian mystery, and it will always be a mystery completely escaping our human categories of understanding, is stated as the Godhead being one, a Nature that remains in its oneness incomprehensible and yet it embraces three Persons: Father in relationship to His Son through His Spirit, the Son in relationship to the Father through the Spirit and the Spirit as the personified Love of the Father and the Son.

What must be avoided is to conceive the Godhead or the Divine Nature as an entity out of which flow three distinct Persons who equally possess this "thingness" of God's essence. Avoiding objectivization of Godhead and the three Divine Persons, we enter into a reverence towards God's mysterious manner of "being" within Himself.

St. Augustine shows us the necessity of keeping "talk" about the Trinity always in the context of mutual relations to each of the Divine Persons. He insists that what is predicated of the Persons is not predicated of them in themselves but only in relation to each other (and also creatures).[16] These relations within the Father's communion between His Word in His Spirit are what distinguish the Persons from each other and prevents them from being reduced to each other as subordinated functions.[17] Jesus Christ revealed while on earth this essential mystery of the Father communicating Himself to us through the Son and the Spirit. "To have seen me is to have seen the Father . . . I am in the Father and the Father is in me" (Jn 14:9, 10). He also revealed that only through the Holy Spirit can we come to know the Son and all He is to the Father. "When the Advocate comes whom I shall send to you from the Father, the Spirit of truth who issues from the Father, he will be my witness" (Jn 15:26; also Jn 14:17, 26; 16:14).

There can be no Father, therefore, but as revealed through His Son. There can be no Son relationship except in relation to the Father that begets Him eternally. And such a begetting and being a begotten cannot be possible except as manifested through the Spirit of Love.

THE REVEALING SON AND SPIRIT

The Godhead that moves toward expression and intelligibility or meaningfulness does so in the relationship of the Godhead as Father knowing Himself in His full Meaning, His Son. This is not only a meaningfulness toward us creatures in the order of salvation, but it is the Son who is the one that, in His eternal "imaging" of the Father's love through the Holy Spirit, gives to the Godhead as Father His full meaning. The Father knows Himself only in His image, His Son. The Godhead concentrates His entire essence in the Son that allows the Father to become the knower and the Son as known, but also vice versa, the Son in the Spirit is the knower as He knows the Father to be His total Source and Origin of being and the Father is known as Father.

But this inter-relationship between the Father and Son in self-knowledge cannot be possible except through the Holy Spirit. This is why there must be a triple movement within the one Godhead. It is the Holy Spirit who eternally illumines the Mystery for the Father and the Son. St. Hilary of Poitiers insists that the Father and the Son have a perfect, mutual knowledge, which exists because of their mutual relationship of Father and Son to each other.[18] If the Father and Son mutually know themselves, this is brought about necessarily by the Holy Spirit that allows them not only mutually to affirm themselves as Father and Son but mutually to recognize themselves as such. The Father and Son, knowing themselves in that primal act of "emptying" of the Father into the Son and the Son "emptying" of Himself into the Father in mutual self-surrender is nothing but the binding force of the Holy Spirit as Love. The Holy Spirit cannot be an accidental relation, a "thing" produced, even from all eternity, but in a mysterious manner the Holy Spirit unites the Father and Son eternally in love that cannot be separated from the knowing by the Father in His Son. The Spirit makes it possible that the unity of the Godhead can be still shared without destroying that unity in the diversity of Persons who share in that essence.

From this three-fold movement, therefore, all reality within the Trinity and without, i.e. in the order of creation and God's shared being through His uncreated energies of love, flows. The Divine Logos is the natural and perfect expression of the Father and is naturally and perfectly expressed by the Love of the Father that is the Spirit. Knowledge is not enough but it must be completed by love since it exists in that first movement of self-giving. Love completes the knowledge and, although knowledge and love are not the same, within the Trinity both the Son as known in the love of the Father and as knowing the Father in His returned love can be possible only through realized love which is the Spirit proceeding from the Father along with Son. Yet both proceed differently from the one Source.

AN UNCHANGING MOVEMENT

This eternal movement within the Trinity is totally an immanent action that knows no finite beginning, increase or cessation. It is an eternal "insession" or, to use the word coined by the early Greek Fathers, a "perichoresis." It is a relational inter-penetration of all three Persons, distinct by their oppositional relationships. Yet all are one in the very knowing and loving that each possesses the same nature.

This "perichoresis" in knowledge and love, in unity and distinction, is the basis for God's trinitarian "inter-penetration" within us human beings as the trinitarian indwelling, as will be developed later. God's humility in sharing His being with us human beings is to be found in His humble, "homely" love, to quote Julian of Norwich's striking phrase. This "homely" love is God calling us into His very own family, God's *home.* To make His home with us is to take us into His very own "family." He allows us to participate in His very own nature as 2 P 1:4 says.

Within the Trinity, therefore, because of God's humility in wanting to know and love Himself in His Son and Spirit we find the basis of all reality. Love becomes energized love when it is an actualized sharing of one's being with another. True love always is rooted in humble self-giving. And thus, at the heart of all reality in the Christian view is the eternal Father wanting to have no being except in His begetting into being His eternal Son. Panikkar has caught this thought in what he terms "the Cross in the Trinity":

> In the Father the apophatism (the *kenosis* or emptying) of Being is real and total. This is what elsewhere I have called 'the Cross in the Trinity' i.e. the integral immolation of God, of which the Cross of Christ and his immolation are only the images and revelations.[19]

If Jesus Christ, the Word of God incarnate and perfect image of the Heavenly Father in human form, became that perfect expression of the Father's love both for Himself and for all of us loved by the Father in His Word, then we can understand how His awesome *kenosis* on the Cross tells us something of the Father's self-giving within the Trinity, the basis of all true self-giving and the energies of love, grace, that make all human loves and self-givings possible.

LOVE IS EMPTYING

St. Paul gives us in his letter to the Philippians an early Christian hymn that exalts the humility of Jesus by His undergoing in obedience to the Father the death on a cross:

> His state was divine,
> yet he did not cling
> to his equality with God
> but emptied himself

to assume the condition of a slave,
and became as men are;
and being as all men are,
he was humbler yet,
even to accepting death,
death on a cross.
But God raised him high
and gave him the name
which is above all other names
so that all beings
in the heavens, on earth and in the underworld,
should bend the knee at the name of Jesus
and that every tongue should acclaim
Jesus Christ as Lord,
to the glory of God the Father (Ph 2:6-11).

Jesus, loved by the Father infinitely, was being driven in His human consciousness, not by any obligation, but by the consuming desire to take His life in His hands and give it back to His beloved Father. In a way we could say that Jesus, given who He was, the Word of the Father made flesh, "had" to pour Himself out or He would have done psychic and spiritual harm to His nature. In emptying Himself by free choices to suffer more and more, Jesus was becoming the Image of His Heavenly Father. He was becoming the manifested Word, God's presence of an infinite love that goes all the way, even unto death, speaking to all of us that for each of us God the Father dies in His perfect image.

As there is both light and darkness in Jesus' *kenosis,* so we can say that in the eternal Father's wish to come out of "non-being" into being by freely wishing to manifest Himself in the meaningfulness of His Word, His Son, there is also darkness mingled with the light. Can we not say, therefore, that Jesus, becoming the Suffering Servant of Yahweh, freely wants to suffer and be poured out as spilt wax only because He wanted His human mind to be the perfect reflection of the Divine Mind? His human consciousness was to become one with the consciousness of the Father. Jesus in His service to the world, entering into the very depths of sin and death and utter emptiness of self, was choosing humanly to be like God. It was the most perfect plan of imaging the eternal love of the Father both for His Son through His Holy Spirit and for all of us born by the Spirit of Jesus into a oneness with the Father's only begotten Son.

We have no way of knowing the Father but through the Son. In Jesus Christ we not only see the perfect human expression of the eternal Word-Son of the Father, but we also see the image of the Godhead, as it moves eternally to express its fullness in love to His Son. The Father must be in His imaged-Word. The Word has meaning only because He is the exact image of the Father who is communicating Himself in His Word.

Gerald Vann, O.P. expresses the immutability of the Godhead and the changeability in His Word made flesh:

> Of the human body of Christ you can say that first it suffered, and then it was glorified and made glad; but throughout that temporal sequence the Godhead remains unchanged, and unchanged precisely in its knowledge and willing of, and its will to share in, that which Christ on the Cross took to himself and made his own and in his glorification turned into glory.[20]

SELF-DIFFUSIVE

St. Bonaventure, very much in the Eastern Fathers' tradition, especially as found in the writings of Pseudo-

Dionysius, went beyond St. Thomas who insisted that
God's nature is, *He Who Is.* The Seraphic Doctor wrote
that Goodness is the name that best describes the Trinity as
the Father, Son and Spirit, one in nature, pour themselves
out differently on behalf of each other.[20]

Thus in summary of what has been developed in this
chapter, we have seen how the unexpressed Godhead is
beyond all being and hence all relationships. It is when
God's nature as *one* moves toward self-giving that God
takes on the personal relationship that is called Father.
This is God's holiness as He moves toward His Son to have
His being in knowing Himself in His Son. God's holiness
becomes expressed to Himself as self-giving Father to His
Son through His personalized love, the Holy Spirit.

We cannot understand the "economic" relationships
of our Heavenly Father to us in Christ Jesus through His
Holy Spirit except first by understanding well that the
Father is self-diffusiveness toward His Son. Only because
this primal relation within the Trinity is true is there the
basis for similar triune action toward a created world and
us creatures.

When Jesus revealed to us: "The Father Himself loves
you" (Jn 16:27), He was revealing the essence of God as
Father, knowing and loving His Son in His Spirit through
self-communion, the sharing of Himself totally with
Another, His Son.

By faith we can believe the Good News that Jesus
makes possible by His Holy Spirit: " . . . and my Father
will love him, and we shall come to him and make our
home with him" (Jn 14:23). If the Father dwells in us He
loves us in Jesus. In His Spirit of love He continually is
begetting us into the likeness of His beloved Son. He does
not call us His children in any extrinsic fashion. But He

transforms us into new creatures in Christ Jesus (2 Co 5:17). This is the mystery that amazes St. John the Evangelist when he writes:

> Think of the love that the Father has lavished on us,
> by letting us be called God's children;
> and that is what we are.
> . . . My dear people, we are already the children of God
> but what we are to be in the future
> has not yet been revealed . . . (1 Jn 3:1-2).

The Good News that Jesus reveals to us is that the Father's love is a self-giving that seeks to be a constant presence of fidelity. He wishes not merely to communicate truths about Himself, but He wishes to share a deep communion of Himself, His very own *being* with us. This God, personalized in three relationships and yet always one in nature as love poured out, seeks to be so present to us that He lives within us. His total being, in His uncreated energies, surrounds us, possesses us, lives immanently within us. We are being "invaded" constantly by an outpouring God. Praise the humility of God that places God within us in a state of constant self-giving to us. We can now move toward the Son and the Holy Spirit, the "two hands of God" in the phrase of St. Irenaeus, that come at us as processions out of the Fatherhood to actuate God as our Father and us as His children in Christ Jesus through His Holy Spirit.

4

The Son and the Holy Spirit

We have been made for communion, a "union with" God and fellow human beings. Another way of putting it is to describe God as love and we, through His abiding, loving presence dwelling within us and inside of each event of each day, are to receive His loving energies and thus live in communion with all persons we meet. We begin to move toward loving communion by means of "communication."

Communication is the first step in becoming "present" to another. In such language we relay information to another on a linear level. Such knowledge tends to be logical, facts, ideas that are comprehensible to our human reasoning. Our sciences are examples of such communication. We go to school to receive knowledge of facts. Our lives depend upon such knowledge. But there is a higher level of knowledge. This is communion between friends and lovers, between ourselves and our loving God. It is the language of the human heart in which love speaks and makes the loved one *present* as a gift to the other. There can be no array of logical proofs that will even bring about such a communion. It is a surrendering love built upon faith and hope in the one loved.

In loving another, we become a gifted presence to that person. We wish to live in union (the true meaning of "communion") with that person so as to be present as often as possible, not only physically in space and time, but more importantly in the inner recesses of our consciousness. We become present to each other in deeper and deeper consciousness to the degree that we can share our most intimate thoughts through speech. An often repeated "I love you," is not giving new, logical information, but it is moving toward communion. We need words as the most ordinary way of communicating our inner self as gift to the other. Without internal words that can be expressed in externalized words, spoken or written or acted out in gestures, we would never grow in love.

But we human beings are this way because God is this way in His essence as Love. God the Father, in absolute silence, in a communication of love impossible for us human beings to understand, speaks His one eternal Word through His Spirit of Love. In that one Word, the Father is perfectly present, totally self-giving to His Son. "In him lives the fullness of divinity" (Col 2:9).

But in His Spirit, the Father also hears His Word come back to Him in a perfect, eternal "yes" of total surrendering Love that is again the Holy Spirit. The Trinity is a reciprocal community of a movement of the Spirit of Love between Father and Son. Our weak minds cannot fathom the peace and joy, the ardent excitement and exuberant self-surrender that flow in a reposeful motion between Father and Son through the Holy Spirit. God becomes real only because He can communicate in Love with His Word. His Word gives Him His identity as Father. But that means eternal self-giving to the Other, His Word in Love, the Holy Spirit.

Before we can understand how this trinitarian move-ment indwells us and sweeps us up into an unchanging, always freshly new action of divine self-giving in the deepest communion possible to us human beings, we must seek to understand what revelation has given us about the inner trinitarian life, about the relationships that exist within the Trinity between the Father with His Son and Holy Spirit. Only by understanding how God com-municates within His own family can we understand the communion that is possible through grace.

INTER-PERSONAL RELATIONS

One of the key models used in trinitarian theology, both in the East and the West, is that proposed and developed in detail by St. Augustine and repeated by St. Thomas Aquinas. It has been called the "psychological image" of the Trinity found within the very reflective pro-cess of the human person concerning his own con-sciousness. St. Augustine describes this analogy: "For we both are, and know that we are, and delight in our being, and know our knowledge of it."[1] The Father is the Source of being, the Son is associated with the Father's knowing of Himself in His Word and the Spirit in the love of the Father knowing Himself in His Word. K. Rahner and a host of modern theologians find this model quite inade-quate to express the dynamic inter-personal relations that exist between Father, Son and Holy Spirit.[2] H. Mühlen finds this model's inadequacy to consist in its weakness to explain the spiration of the Holy Spirit.[3]

Perhaps a model proposed by Richard of St. Victor (+ 1173) can serve to avoid the scholastic language of view-ing the inner trinitarian relations in a static manner and put us in touch with a more biblical and Greek patristic approach. We can relate deeply to this model as it is built upon the mystery of love relationships. Richard bases his understanding of the Trinity on the premise that true love seeks to be totally self-sacrificing on behalf of the one loved. But such a love wants to be shared with another, thus an *I* and *Thou* move into a *We*-community of three persons equally loving each other with the very same love. He writes:

> When one gives love to another and when he alone loves the other alone, there is love certainly but not shared love. When two love each other and give each other their most ardent affection and when the affection of the first flows to the second and that of the second to the first, moving as it were in different directions, there is love on both sides certainly, but there is not shared love. Strictly speaking, there is shared love when two persons love a third in a harmony of affection and a community of love and when the loves of the two converge in the single flame of love they have for the third . . . From this, then, it is evident that shared love would not have a place in the divinity if there were only two persons and not a third.[4]

Whatever human words may be used to penetrate somewhat the inner mystery of God's nature as love in a communion of persons, our attitude demands something of the apophatic approach of the early Eastern Fathers who learned so well from Holy Scripture and from their own sense of brokenness in prayer that only God can lead us into this mystery. We must realize that we cannot comprehend God's inner life completely or we would have to be part of that Godly family by our very nature. Yet Scripture insists that we can know this Trinity by not knowing

Him. In our poverty and utter creatureliness, in our sinfulness and alienation from the Father, we realize that to know God is beyond our power. "No one has ever seen God; it is the only Son, who is nearest to the Father's heart, who has made him known" (Jn 1:18). Yet we can come to know the Father through the revelation of the Son: "And eternal life is this: to know you, the only true God, and Jesus Christ whom you have sent" (Jn 17:3).

As we Christians grow in contemplation, we realize more and more that God must reveal Himself to us. Man can only wait in the desert of his nothingness, hoping to receive God as He wishes to make Himself known. With the humility of children we seek entrance into the heart of God as He communicates Himself to His Word through His Spirit of love. This is the teaching of Jesus who speaks about the possibility of such children receiving not merely knowledge or a communication but the privilege in contemplation to enter into the very trinitarian "communion."

> I bless you, Father, Lord of heaven and of earth, for hiding these things from the learned and the clever and revealing them to mere children. Yes, Father, for that is what it pleased you to do. Everything has been entrusted to me by my Father; and no one knows the Son except the Father, just as no one knows the Father except the Son and those to whom the Son chooses to reveal him (Mt 11:25-27).

THE DIVINE WORD

From the revealed word of God in the Old and New Testaments and in the living tradition of the Church through the centuries, the Divine Nature is considered as inaccessible, uncommunicable to man. This is the awesome, transcendent God of majesty appearing to Moses at the burning bush, the God of Isaias' vision who receives the constant praise of the Trisagion from the six-winged Seraphim who cover their faces with their wings out of reverence.

Etienne Gilson has expressed this foundation-stone for all of our human relationships with God:

> Lower even if only for an instant and at one given point the abyss between God and man created by the contingency of creaturehood and you have taken away from the Christian mystic his God and hence his mysticism also. Any God who is not inaccessible, man can dispense with. It is the God who is by His nature inaccessible whom man cannot do without.[5]

Nietzsche put it this way: "The God that I can understand ceases to interest me."

Yet Jesus Christ promises us that this inaccessible God with the life of the Trinity will descend and enter into our very beings. "If anyone loves me he will keep my word, and my Father will love him, and we shall come to him and make our home with him" (Jn 14:23). Jesus Christ is the Word and the Son of the Father. He is the way, the truth and the life that brings us into the awesome mystery of the Trinity as a communion in its own life. All other names applied to the Word and the Son, such as Image, Wisdom, Light and Life etc. are summarized in these two central names.

The Word of God is found in Holy Scripture and in the Church's liturgical prayers as referring to the Second Person of the Trinity. The Greek Fathers knew that any discussion of the inaccessible God and the immanent union with His creature-man must start with the Divine Logos, with the Word of God inside the Trinity. This is the Speech of God in His divine, eternal existence that allows God to move in His spoken or pronounced Word outside of the inner-trinitarian life in the created world.

The Johannine Gospel powerfully speaks of God's eternal Word:

> In the beginning was the Word:
> the Word was with God
> and the Word was God.
> He was with God in the beginning.
> Through him all things came to be . . . (Jn 1:1-2).

This Divine Word became flesh and "pitched His tent among us" (Jn 1:14). It is He therefore, who can reveal to us that the Father is known to Himself and to us in and through His very Word. "He is known by the name, The Word of God" (Rv 19:13). St. Ignatius of Antioch describes how God manifests Himself through His Word: "There is one God, who manifested himself through Jesus Christ his Son, who is His Word proceeding from silence."[6] This Word is the perfect image of the invisible God (Col 1:15). He is the thought of the Father that contains all the knowledge that the Father has of Himself and of His eternal Son and of all things in that Word. "He is the radiant light of God's glory and the perfect copy of his nature . . . " (Heb 1:3).

Holy Scripture teaches us in the words of Jesus Christ that the Word of God receives all its force and power from the Father. He is the perfect reflection of the Mind that speaks this word.

The Son can do nothing by himself;
he can do only what he sees the Father doing:
and whatever the Father does, the Son does too (Jn 5:19).

And again Jesus says: "And my word is not my own: it is the word of the one who sent me" (Jn 14:24). He can do nothing of Himself. The truth and judgment that He renders is that which the Father pours into Him (Jn 5:30). He is Light from Light. He is not in some sense God but He is God's Word.

The Eastern Fathers, especially those who had been educated in the Greek paideia,[7] such as Clement of Alexandria, Origen, St. Athanasius and the Cappadocian Fathers, Sts. Basil, Gregory of Nazianzus and Gregory of Nyssa, often used the concept of Logos found in the Greek philosophies of Heraclitus and the Stoics but especially in the religious speculation of Philo (+44 A.D.). For the Greeks in general, Logos "means not only the side of God which is reflected in creation, which touches the finite world, it is the ultimate reason which explains all existence, the eternal principle that underlies phenomena."[8]

Logos becomes Wisdom personified in the Book of *Proverbs,* for example: "From everlasting I was firmly set, from the beginning, before earth came into being . . . I was by his side, a master craftsman, delighting him day after day, ever at play in his presence, at play everywhere in his world, delighting to be with the sons of men" (Pr 8:23-31).

ST. ATHANASIUS

It was St. Athanasius more than all other early Fathers who developed a theology of the Logos made flesh in Jesus Christ to be *homoousios,* of the same nature as the Father. The theology of St. Athanasius, who combated the heresy of Arianism that claimed Jesus to have been mere man, adopted as the son of God, but not the pre-existent Logos from all eternity, became the turning point for the development of the orthodox teaching on the Trinity. Hence we see his doctrine of Logos as an important element in church teaching.

St. Athanasius asks the questions of his adversaries:

> If there be an Image of the invisible God, it is an invisible Image; nay, I will be bold to add, that, as being the likeness of the Father, never was it not. For when was that God, who, according to John, is called Light (for 'God is Light'), without a radiance of His proper glory, that a man should presume to assert the Son's origin of existence, as if before He was not? But when was not that Image of the Father's Ineffable and Nameless and Unutterable Subsistence, that Expression and Word, and He that knows the Father? For let him understand well who dares to say, 'Once the Son was not,' that he is saying, 'Once Wisdom was not,' and 'Word was not,' and 'Life was not.'⁹

St. Athanasius, unlike St. Irenaeus who employed the Logos doctrine to show the Incarnate Logos as the invisible God made visible, used the Logos doctrine as the Image of the Father, having no immediate relationship to the created order in order to conclude that therefore He is like the Father in the same essence. The Church accepted this teaching that Jesus Christ is truly the pre-existent Logos, one with the Father in the very same divine nature. But the Logos doctrine was too abstract to enter into the living piety of Christians. It was a doctrine developed to prove the full divinity of Jesus Christ as one person with the eternal, pre-existent Word of God.

THE SON

The term *Logos* had an appeal in the early Chuch for those educated in philosophy. But the term *Son* was more frequently applied to Jesus Christ by the faithful as well as by the Fathers of the Church. And this for two main reasons. First, Jesus Himself in the words of the New Testament and in the Liturgy is referred to as the Son of God more frequently than as the Word of God.

This faith in the Son of God is formulated clearly in the profession of faith of the Council of Constantinople (381 A.D.).

I believe in God, the Father Almighty,
in one Lord, Jesus Christ,
only Son of God,
born of the Father before all ages,
God of God, Light of Light,
true God of true God,
engendered, not created,
of one substance with the Father.

St. John presents the Son as the expressed love of the Father for us: "Yes, God loved the world so much that he gave his only Son so that everyone who believes in him may not be lost but may have eternal life. For God sent his Son into the world . . . so that through him the world might be saved" (Jn 3:16-17; also Jn 4:9).

In God's revelation, of all the titles given to the Second Person within the Trinity, the one of *Son* was deemed

by God to lead us best into the inner trinitarian mystery.
For this reason St. John's Gospel could call the Son "the
Way, the Truth and the Life" (Jn 14:6). The Godhead
knows itself in its Logos, the perfect expression of the
Eternal Mind. But when Scripture reveals to us that God is
a Father who gives Himself completely in the begetting of
His only begotten Son, then we are moved to new
knowledge. God does more than know Himself in His
Image. He empties Himself in self-giving and mutual shar-
ing with His Son.

> For the Father, who is the source of life
> has made the Son the source of life (Jn 5:26).

Of all New Testament writings we find most clearly in
St. John's Gospel the Father and Son relationship
described for us. Jesus never links Himself with us in a
commonly shared sonship. He reveals that His sonship is
unique. "I am ascending to my Father and your Father, to
my God and your God" (Jn 20:17).

THE UNIQUE SON OF THE FATHER

John's Gospel clearly brings to a fulfillment what was
hinted at in the frequent use in the Synoptic Gospels of the
title of "Son of Man." Twice in the prologue of John's
Gospel Jesus Christ is referred to as the "only Son"
(*monogenes*) of the eternal Father. This man of Nazareth
claims to exist before Abraham, when He uses the verb
that Yahweh used to reveal the Godhead to Moses (Ex
3:14): "I tell you most solemnly, before Abraham ever
was, *I Am*" (Jn 8:58). He is a person who has come "from

above" (Jn 8:23), " . . . the Son of Man who is in heaven" (Jn 3:13).

He speaks of what He has seen with "my Father" (Jn 8:38). And the Jewish "religionists" understand clearly His revelation and seek to stone Him for seeking to make Himself God (Jn 10:33). Clearly we know the Father has a Son because He sent His Son into this world not to judge but to save it (Jn 3:17). Knowledge of the Son is as important as knowledge of the Father in order to obtain eternal life (Jn 17:3). The Son confesses that He is not independent of His Father but He depends totally upon Him as His Source.

> I tell you most solemnly, the Son can do nothing by himself; he can do only what he sees the Father doing and whatever the Father does the Son does too. For the Father loves the Son and shows him everything he does himself (Jn 5:19-20; cf. also: Jn 6:57; 8:29; 12:49; 17:1 f.)

The Father is greater than the Son (Jn 14:28) since everything that the Son has, has come to Him from the Father as from His Source. Jesus is in the Father and the Father is in Him (Jn 14:10). One has only to see Jesus and he sees the Father. In the whole Johannine Last Supper Discourse (Jn 14-17) we see an outpouring of the heart of Jesus revealing to us the intimate relationships between His Father and Himself. The doctrine of grace would be culled from such a revelation. We can see how most important it is to ground ourselves on this basic revelation of the Trinity from Scripture in order to extend those intratrinitarian relationships into our own divine filiation with the Father through the Son in His Spirit.

Thus we can believe with certain knowledge that the

Father begets eternally His only begotten Son through His Spirit of love. He gives Him His very substance, not partially as in human generation, but His total *being*, all except His very Fatherhood. Since the Son is one in substance with the Father, He, through the Incarnation, can bring us not only to a knowledge of the Father but He can actualize ourselves through His Holy Spirit into children of God, sharing in His very own nature (2 P 1:4). St. Athanasius, quoting St. Irenaeus, could summarize the end of the Incarnation: "For He was made man that we might be made God."[10]

THE SPIRIT OF GOD

But if there were only the Father and the Son, there would be no community of two Persons giving themselves to each other and fructifying in a third. There would be no movement outside of a mutual desire toward *union*. The result would be not only a denial of the Trinity but a negation of a God who has so loved us as to give us His only begotten Son so that in His Gift, the Spirit of love, we might have eternal life (Jn 3:16).

Richard of St. Victor shows that God must enjoy the highest degree of love, agape, since God is perfect goodness. But true love in its perfect manifestation is a love that moves away from self to communicate itself to another. Any love that does not go beyond itself is still imperfect.[11] But in God such another person to whom God gives Himself cannot be a created person since God would be loving that person infinitely and perfectly but in an inordinate way. The loveableness of the second person would have to be in proportion to God's love. The Second Person of the Trinity, for Richard, is that "co-worthy" person and, therefore, He Himself is also God. Thus it seems as though perfect love would demand at least two divine Persons of equal worth.

But true love is driven to a transcendence that wants love received to be shared by a third person. Richard argues for the existence within the Trinity of the Holy Spirit on the basis of the psychology of love. The Son wants to love the Father with a perfect mutual love just as the Father loves Him.[12] It would be an imperfection between the Father and the Son if their love did not want to be shared with another. But to share this mutual love there is need of a *condilectum,* one that is loved equally as the Father loves the Son and the Son loves the Father. This is the Holy Spirit.[13]

The parallel with human love found in marriage could be a most powerful argument from experience for the Trinity. As the Father and Son wish to perfect their love by sharing it with the Third Person, the Holy Spirit, so do a husband and wife wish to fashion a community of at least three by a child. Two in love move toward union, but only in the sharing of their mutual love with a third person does their union become fulfilled. This parallel is found also in God's salvific designs on the human race, beginning with His Chosen People. His perfect love outside of the Trinity is a reflection of that community of love not only desiring union with His People but actually effecting a union in the fashioning of a third entity that can share their love. God's love for the human race would be incomplete if He would not by grace wish to share His very own love and life by making us His children through the Incarnate Son and Holy Spirit.

Today there is a great stress being placed on interpersonal relations. Father Heribert Mühlen has brought about an exciting synthesis of the insights of past theologians, such as St. Augustine, Richard of St. Victor, St. Thomas Aquinas and Duns Scotus, to highlight the inter-personal relationships within the Trinity.[14] Mühlen takes many insights from the metaphysics of language as done by Dietrich von Hildebrand[15] and Wilhelm von Humboldt[16] in order to show the distinctive personality of the Holy Spirit as coming out of an I-Thou relationship between Father and Son.

Before we move into such a description of the Holy Spirit in terms of interpersonal relationships, so necessary if we are to enter into a deep experiential knowledge and love of the indwelling Trinity, let us see some of the past difficulties that concern the Holy Spirit, especially those coming from Holy Scripture. Surely for most of us there is little difficulty in understanding the Son-relationship, both from Holy Scripture and dogmatically within the Trinity itself. This Son has become incarnate and has spoken about Himself. In regard to the Father, the Son has revealed to us what He is like. Added to this revelation, we have a "natural" revelation of such an I-Thou relationship in our natural existence of being sons and daughters of an earthly father and mother.

But when we seek to probe more deeply into the meaning of the Holy Spirit, both within the Trinity and within our own spiritual life, we find many difficulties. Historically in the great ecumenical councils the dogma about the divinity of the Holy Spirit and His relationship with the Father and Son had been articulated after the great Christological dogmas had been clarified. This no doubt is due to the lack of clarity found in Holy Scripture. But it also means that a doctrine that depends totally upon other doctrines cannot be clarified until such prior doctrines have been clearly enunciated. The implications of the Holy Spirit could have been drawn only when the full divinity of the Son, of the same nature as of the Father, an equal I-Thou community, was firmly established.

SPIRIT IN THE OLD TESTAMENT

In the Old Testament, Spirit (in Hebrew *ruah*) referred to the breath of life. Yahweh, who was the Source of all that lived, was pre-eminently "alive" and was called the Spirit. The name also referred to the mighty power of the wind and suggested the destructive power of Yahweh (Ps 29:8; 1 Kgs 19:11) or His creative power as in Ps. 3:6 and Ezk 37:9 f. Men were given new hearts by God's Spirit (Ezk 36:26). This Spirit would transform barrenness into fertile land.

> Once more there will be poured on us the Spirit from above; then shall the wilderness be fertile and the fertile land becomes forest (Is 32:15).

God has prophesied that the living presence of His Spirit among His people would be poured out in a future age in great abundance:

> I will pour out my spirit on all mankind.
> Your sons and daughters shall prophesy,
> your old men shall dream dreams,
> and your young men see visions.
> Even on the slaves, men and women,
> will I pour out my spirit in those days (Jl 3:1-2).

The Spirit of God is, therefore, seen in the Old Testament as a presence of God, stirring men to a deeper relationship with Him. That presence is not far away, yet it cannot be seen. It can only be experienced—but only by those who search out that presence. "When you seek me you shall find me, when you seek me with all your heart" (Jr 29:13).

SPIRIT IN THE NEW TESTAMENT

As we read the New Testament, we find the Spirit of God relating to Jesus in two distinct ways. Usually in the Synoptic Gospels, the Spirit has priority. He comes upon Jesus and anoints Him. Jesus is first conceived by the power of God's Spirit, is baptized and anointed for His mission by the Spirit. He is driven into the desert by the Spirit. He casts out demons by the Spirit's power, heals and performs all sorts of miracles in the power of the Spirit.[17] Although the Spirit is still presented in a mysterious manner, nevertheless, to Him is attributed the mission and message of Jesus given Him to do by the Father, to make mankind holy and perfect as the Father is.

In the Pauline and Johannine writings we find a different manner of the Spirit-to-Jesus relationship. Not only does Jesus receive the Spirit, but He sends the Holy Spirit upon His followers. The Spirit is the Spirit of Christ or of the Son (Rm 8:9; 2 Co 3:17; Ga 4:6; Ph 1:19). He is also the Spirit of the Father (Rm 8:9a). Jesus promises that "I will send Him (the Advocate) to you" (Jn 16:7). This is the fulfillment of the meaning of God's Spirit in Holy Scripture. Jesus could not give the Spirit until He had died, St. John observes (Jn 7:39). He had first to receive God's

Spirit before He could share God's Spirit with others. He who was the image of the Father first had to receive in His human life the immense love of God. Then He, dying by the power of so great a love for us, could release that same love within our hearts.

The Holy Spirit is sent by Jesus to complete His work on earth (Jn 14:26). The Holy Spirit brings us into the filiation of children of God (Rm 8:15; Ga 4:6). The Spirit, however, is a creative force that is new and distinct from Jesus. He is a special power different from the power of Jesus. Yet He is tied to Jesus Christ. "We know that He lives in us by the Spirit that He has given us" (1 Jn 3:24). The Holy Spirit is presented as the new way of existence and action by the Risen Jesus.[18] Jesus is the New Adam. He is the first fruits, the first-born of many sons. Risen, Jesus is what the whole world is to become. The Spirit's work is to be Christ's life-giving Spirit to the world. He draws us into Christ, into His Body. He divinizes us, making us "new creatures" in Christ Jesus (2 Co 5:17).

When Jesus' human body is glorified by the Father's Spirit, it becomes for all of us the source of the Spirit, of eternal life. Now Jesus Risen cannot be separated from His Spirit. The Spirit is God's life-giving "Breath" that the Risen Jesus is always breathing upon us. Thus we can see why St. John tells us that Jesus could not have given His Spirit before He had died (Jn 7:39).

AN I-THOU-WE COMMUNITY

The greatest deterrent in presenting the Holy Spirit as the transforming love of the Father and the Son that divinizes us into the very community of the Trinity came, however, through the scholastic presentation both of the

Holy Spirit and the Trinity. The four Aristotelian categories to explain any causality (material, formal, efficient and final causes) were used to explain both the actions of the Trinity outside of itself toward the created world and also to describe the operations of the individual Persons indwelling us through created grace. Created grace, as habitual and sanctifying, was objectivized away from the personal love relationships of the trinitarian Persons towards us.

Mühlen helps us to recapture the insights of Holy Scripture, especially the Hesed Covenant, and allows us also to interpret grace primarily, as the Greek Fathers did, as the uncreated energies of the total God-community meeting us individuals with the individuated, personalized relationships of each trinitarian Person as found within that Trinity-community. Using the insight of von Humboldt,[19] that speech can arise only through the mediation of a duality, Mühlen shows how the Father and the Son say an *I* and a *Thou* relationship. We have pointed out how the Father knows Himself in His Word and Son and the Son knows Himself only in the Father. The Holy Spirit brings about a *We* relationship.

Dietrich von Hildebrand explains how the *We*-relationship builds upon the I-Thou as the foundation, making the *We*-relationship a community of an I-Thou with a third in a "common performance of acts and attitudes."[20]

The Father not only knows Himself in His Son, but acknowledges Himself as uniquely the Son's Father. The opposition between the Father and Son only increases the intimacy the more each Person acknowledges both His own uniqueness and also that of the Other. Teilhard de Chardin declared that love differentiates as it unites. As the uniqueness of each person increases the intimacy and the desire for greater union, love is generated and brings about the union. But this love cannot be a thing in the Trinity. It must be the personalized Act of Love coming out of the mutual love of the Father and Son, loving each other in "our Spirit." The Spirit "proceeds" from the union of the two, uniquely different Persons, Father and Son. His being as a Person within the Trinity consists in being the act of union and distinction between the Father and Son and in this "action" the Spirit finds His "personality." Thus the Spirit can never be considered apart from either the Father or the Son.

Speaking the Word in eternal silence through His outpouring Love that is His Holy Spirit, the Heavenly Father hears His Word come back to Him in a perfect, eternal, "yes" of total, surrendering Love, that is again the Holy Spirit. The theological controversy between the Orthodox and the Catholic Churches about the *Filioque* (whether the Holy Spirit proceeds from the Father alone or also from the Son) is no controversy when contemplated in the eternal begetting of God's Word in God's Love. Both Churches hold a partial statement of the truth. The contemplative, who stands before this sacred mystery, knows in a knowledge given only by God's Spirit that the Holy Spirit proceeds as Love from the Father and in that same proceeding act of Love the Word is eternally spoken, known and loved. But the Son echoes this Divine Love as He, the Word, goes back to the Father in the same Divine Spirit. The Spirit originates from the Father but through the mediation of the Son that forms the I-Thou community and through the Spirit attains a We-community. The Spirit also proceeds back to the Father as the Word's loving response. The Holy Spirit is the silent gasp of mutual, loving surrender between Father and Son in a community of *We*. He brings to completion the divine union between Father and Son in the ecstasy of shared love.

Thus, understanding the Holy Spirit not as a separate Person within the Trinity, but in the light of the unity and distinction between the Father and the Son, the One who brings about through mutual love the We-community, we can see that we cannot have a personal relationship to the Spirit. It would be more theologically correct not to pray *to* the Spirit, but only pray *in* the Spirit. The Spirit can never be objectivized and spoken to but He must be experienced in the circular movement of love between the Father and Son. Thus we can now move to consider the Trinity in its relationships to the created world, especially to us human beings. Only in such a We-community, brought about by the personalized act of Love between Father and Son, that is the Holy Spirit, can we envision God as a unity, yet enjoying all three personalized acts within the Trinity, moving outwardly to share His We-community.

It is this moving of God's We-community towards mankind in order to give man a share in the life of the Three Persons that is at the heart of the Christian message. St. Paul, similar to the other New Testament writers, never gives us a clear, abstract statement of the Trinity in terms of nature, persons, *circuminsession,* created grace and so many other terms that theologians have developed through the centuries in order to clarify this fundamental mystery of God's inner Being and His relations with us. St. Paul's statement in the first chapter of his letter to the Ephesians can serve to summarize in non-speculative, theological terms or rather in scriptural terms, the movement of this we-community into our world in order to share with us human beings the same relationships enjoyed between Father and Son as I-Thou, brought together in perfect, loving union by the Spirit who fashions and is fashioned a *We*-community that in God's holiness and humility stretches down to engulf us also into that We-community through the Body of Christ in His Spirit.

Blessed be God the Father of our Lord Jesus Christ,
who has blessed us with all the spiritual blessings of heaven
   in Christ.
Before the world was made, he chose us, chose us in
   Christ,
to be holy and spotless, and to live through love in his
   presence,
determining that we should become his adopted sons,
   through Jesus Christ
. . . to make us praise the glory of his grace,
his free gift to us in the Beloved . . .
He has let us know the mystery of his purpose,
the hidden plan he so kindly made in Christ from the
   beginning . . .
that he would bring everything together under Christ, as
   head,
everything in the heavens and everything on earth.
. . . Now you too, in him,
have heard the message of the truth and the good news of
   your salvation,
and have believed it;
and you too have been stamped with the seal of the Holy
   Spirit of the Promise,
the pledge of our inheritance
which brings freedom for those whom God has taken for
   his own,
to make his glory praised (Ep 1:3-14).

5

Invaded by God

Batter my heart, three-personed God; for You
as yet but knock, breathe, shine and seek to mend;
That I may rise, and stand, o'erthrow me, and bend
Your force, to break, blow, burn and make me new.
I, like an usurped town, to another due,
Labor to admit You, but oh! to no end;
Reason, Your viceroy in me, me should defend,
But is captived and proves weak or untrue.
Yet dearly I love You, and would be loved fain,
But am betrothed to Your enemy.
Divorce me, untie, or break that knot again,
Take me to you, imprison me, for I
except You enthrall me, never shall be free;
Nor even chaste, except you ravish me.

John Donne

Only if God ravish us shall we be what God created us
to be. In the words of St. Irenaeus of the second century,
we are empty receptacles to be filled by God. God first
freely creates us; then freely He seeks to communicate
Himself to us as intellectual beings capable of hearing His
Word. All this is in order that He may share His very
trinitarian life with us.

Yet how we poor human beings will do just about anything to avoid surrendering to God's pervading loving presence! We fear to enter into God's burning love, because, if we do, we know we must *die*. We must allow His consuming love to destroy all vestige of self-centeredness. He alone must become God for us. We must live only for Him and in Him alone we shall find our true being.

But before that surrender to God's supremacy over us, what an agony of resistance we put up. Nikos Kazantzakis describes it: "God is fire and you must walk on it . . . dance on it. At that moment the fire will become cool water. But until you reach that point, what a struggle, my Lord, what agony!"

LORD, THAT I MAY SEE!

We were meant, as Adam and Eve before the fall, to walk through this world and commune with God. We should be able to see God in the rain drop, in the soft colors of the evening sunset, in the thunder and lightning, in snow and frost, in heat and cold. But we do not. We are not in touch with God's energetic love that assumes millions of concrete manifestations surrounding us at every moment, even though He is touching us with His millions of fingers.

The poet and the mystic can still see Him. Gerard Manley Hopkins saw the world as "charged with the grandeur of God. It will flame out, like shining from shook foil . . . " Yet man through greedy commerce has bleared his eyes and fails to see this grandeur. Still it is there.

And for all this, nature is never spent;
There lives the dearest freshness deep down things;

And though the last lights off the black West went
Oh, morning, at the brown brink eastward, springs—
Because the Holy Ghost over the bent
    World broods with warm breast and with ah! bright
      wings.[1]

God in His infinite love breaks out of His trinitarian *We*-community to want to share His life with us human beings. We tremble before the awesome holiness, yes, His very humility that must be at the heart of such a free love in our regard.

A GRACEFUL LOVE

Love, in order to exist, in man or God, must always be loving, always pouring itself out from its own abundance, always giving of itself. Tied to the mysterious makeup of God as an *I* that is also a *We*, is God's bursting forth from within His own perfect, circular, loving, self-containment to love us so that we might accept His love and become happy in sharing His own very family-life, that of the Trinity. The nature of God is such that, while being one in essence, it demands a plurality as objects of His love, of His infinite Self-giving. Love is the best word that St. John and any other human being could choose to describe God's relations to man.

God spills out His love in activity in the creation of human beings and the universe, in the Incarnation of His Divine Son, Jesus Christ, in the Redemption by the God-Man of the whole human and subhuman cosmos, in the sanctification and final Parousia through the Holy Spirit. These are all actions of God prompted by the one constant act of love.

St. Irenaeus pictures God as coming toward us in the created world through His two hands, Jesus Christ and the Holy Spirit.

> And therefore throughout all time, man, having been moulded at the beginning by the hands of God, that is, of the Son and the Spirit, is made after the image and likeness of God.[2]

The Greek Fathers carefully distinguish between the essence of God that is one nature, equally shared by the three Divine Persons, and God's one nature in the multiplied world of creation. Pseudo-Dionysius describes the movement outwardly toward the created world as a "going forth" of God (*proodos* in Greek). The importance of this distinction[3] is rooted in God's revelation. His essence no human being can see or comprehend in any human fashion. No man has ever seen God and lived (Ex 33:23; 1 Jn 4:12; Jn 1:18; 6:46).

Yet God lovingly wishes to share His very own being with us. In man's very own creation, as described in *Genesis*, the trinitarian We-community freely decides to make man in a way that he could share in God's life. "Let us make man in our own image, in the likeness of ourselves" (Gn 1:26). God only asks that man open himself to God's many "goings-forth" in which God wishes to communicate His great, personal love for man. In man's constant response to this invitation of God's love consists all his greatness and fulfillment. If he consents by humbling himself to his true ontological place as a creature before his Creator, if he makes himself supple and malleable in the hands of the Divine Artist, God can make of him His chef-d'oeuvre, a true, loving child of God in union with the only Begotten Son, Jesus Christ, co-heir with Him of Heaven forever. It is man's loving in return (always made possible through God's energizing grace) that divinizes us, brings us into a oneness in love so that God truly lives in us by participation.

"God is love and anyone who lives in love lives in God and God lives in him" (1 Jn 4:16). Grace, therefore, is God loving His human creation and deifying it through His activity with human beings who freely choose the Way to the Truth that leads to Life which is Love Personified.

Through the doctrine of God's energies of love, the Trinity as one in essence but now conceived of as "God for us," we can solve the antinomy between a God who cannot in any way be comprehended in His essence and a God who is constantly communicating Himself to us through creation. The end of the created order, as seen by the early Fathers in their theologizing from Holy Scripture, is that God might divinize us through sharing His trinitarian life. This means that we are capable not only of communicating with God in true knowledge but also entering into a loving communion with Him. The experiencing of the divine energies, God the Father, Son and Holy Spirit, acting as one God, makes it possible for us to enter into a mystical union with God.

GOD'S ENERGIES

St. Basil writes that we know God only by means of His actions or energies.

We say that we know our God by His energies. We do not affirm that we can approach the essence itself. His energies

come down to us, but His essence remains unap-
proachable.[4]

God gives Himself to us through His loving actions. But
the importance of understanding the doctrine of God's
energies is that His actions are not *things* God does to us or
on our behalf. God's energetic actions are God as He,
from His one essence, gives Himself to us dynamically.
This is *primarily* what grace is for the Greek Fathers.

Such a distinction presents God as always dynamically
giving Himself to us in order that we might have a share in
His "uncreated" nature as 2 P 1:4 holds out as the aim of
our life. It avoids any static, objectivizing of grace as
primarily a created accident that man can live without. St.
Thomas Aquinas, using Aristotle's categories, defines
grace as the external principle of human actions. "Man
needs a power added to his natural power by grace," wrote
St. Thomas.[5]

What is crucial in this doctrine is that through God's
energies we actually do make contact with the living God.
God is truly love. He must, therefore, want to give us, not
merely a created grace, but Himself as Gift. The energies
are really God and not a created thing. God does give us
Himself directly as He is personalized in His energies.

APPROPRIATION

We come down to the important and crucial point of
this book. If God is a loving *We* community, does He really give Himself to us in a personalized way? If Holy Scripture and the Tradition of the Church present God as
Father, Son and Holy Spirit, a community of oneness in

inter-relationships of a we, then are we capable of entering into such personal relationships with the Trinity? Does God only give us Himself, not as He truly is, but through means of a gift, called created grace? Or does He allow us to know and love Him in relationships of Father, Son and Spirit?

First, we need to understand the term used by theologians from St. Augustine's time, namely, *appropriations*. It refers to our assigning a certain power or quality to one of the three Divine Persons, even though, as we have just said, any action of God is of God's essential energy of love and is common to all three Persons. However, because of a similarity between that given quality and the distinct, personalized relationship within the Trinity certain attributes were assigned by theologians and spiritual writers to individual Persons. Thus power was associated with the Father since He is the Source of the processions of the Son and Holy Spirit. Wisdom was assigned to the Son since He proceeds as the Word and Image of the Father. Goodness was associated with the Holy Spirit since He is the fullness and loving completion of the Trinity and God's Gift to us in whom all gifts are given.[6]

The language of appropriation allows us to discuss the essential divine attributes of the Trinity as found reflected in creation. It also allows us to find reflections of the Trinity in the beliefs of other religions such as Hinduism and Buddhism.[7] But what is important to remember is that such attributes flow from the total, divine essence and are not "personalized" qualities predicated solely to any one of the Persons of the Trinity. To understand what is personal and proper to each member, as St. Bonaventure wrote, Christian faith is required.[8]

In terms of Byzantine theology all actions that flow

from the divine energies are common to all Persons. From our viewpoint, the manifestations of these energies are multiple. From that of the Trinity, there is one, divine energy attributable to the divine essence, therefore, to the common action of all three Persons. St. Gregory Palamas uses the example of the one sun giving off a ray that equally gives warmth, light, life and nourishment.[9]

A COSMIC TRANSFIGURATION

God is not only continually revealing Himself as Love through His manifold energies flowing from the one essence of God, shared equally by all three Persons in the Trinity, but God is also involved within that revelation of Himself as Love to transfigure this universe into a divinized whole, into the Cosmic Christ.[10] Not only human beings but the whole human cosmos is under "the bondage of corruption" (Rm 8:21) and we daily experience that the whole of creation groans and travails in pain together (Rm 8:22).

But we also believe that God truly loves the world He created. "And God saw that it was good!" (Gn 1:18). He has created all things, every atom of matter, in and through His Word, Jesus Christ. God is present inside of all that exists. "For in him we live and move and have our being" (Ac 17:28). These energies of God bathe the whole universe and charge it with His infinite love. Although at times, all around us may seem to be in chaotic confusion and life has "no exit," as Sartre gave as the final judgment of the world, nevertheless, we Christians must be able to touch God in His energies as He reveals Himself to us in these material manifestations. Above all, we must be able to be touched and transformed into godly creatures by grace.

God is not only transcendent, but by His energies He becomes immanently present throughout all of creation. God as love seeks to become more "present" to us through every creature that He gives us. We can say that God becomes truly transcendent, standing infinitely above, apart, outside of the created, finite world precisely because His infinite energies, uncreated acts of love, flowing out from His essence as God, penetrate immanently the whole created world. His energies touch the core of each being and exert a loving attraction to draw all things unto Himself. We human beings especially are being drawn constantly into the very heart of God in order to be divinized and to share the triune life. In God's transcendence and immanence, the dynamism of His energies is an interaction with us human beings, all in order to lead us to a transfiguration whereby we will be truly made sharers in the very life and love of the Holy Trinity.

GOD'S SELF-REVELATION

Michael Schmaus points out that God reveals Himself to us on a vertical and also a horizontal plane. On the vertical level God reveals Himself to us through the created nature and human spirits, that is, we can know God through His presence in creatures of nature but also through His presence operating in our intellectual faculties. He also reveals Himself on this level through Christ, namely, the Divine Word, that becomes flesh and dwells among us (Jn 1:14). God also reveals Himself within the context of our horizontal, historical existence through the creation of the world, the revelation of Jesus Christ, the Incarnate Word, and in the fulfillment of the world.[11]

These two levels cross each other and it is in their inter-relationships of these levels that we come to the "economic" relationships of God, both in His energies, commonly shared by all three Divine Persons, and in the personalized relationships of each Person to the created world. It is precisely in the person of Jesus Christ that we find the Way to enter into this mystery of God's invasion of us and the whole created world, not only by His un-created energies of love but by the unique actions of each Person of the Trinity continuing in an analogous way the basic "immanent" and personalized acts that constitute each Person His unique Self.

We would always have believed that God would touch us and communicate Himself to us only through the energies. We would always have been unable to enter into "personalized" relationships with the Father, different from those of the Son and the Holy Spirit, if it had not been for the Incarnation. For this mystery of the Incarnation reveals to us through the materiality of the human nature of Christ what our own humanity can attain by grace. This dogma of the hypostatic union teaches us that the Second Person of the Trinity who operates equally and conjointly with the other two Persons in all "energetic" actions throughout the universe, acted in the historical horizontal level in a unique manner that reflected somewhat His very own oppositional relationships to the Father and the Holy Spirit within the immanent life of the Trinity. The Person of the Word of God, different from the Father and the Spirit, but not separated, assumed a human nature. This nature did not exist of itself and then was merely added somehow to the Divine Word. In that very act the Word gave existence to His human nature and divinized it.

This humanity had the immortal and incorruptible character of the nature of Adam before he sinned, yet Jesus Christ in that humanity was·subjected to the conditions of our own fallen natures, as St. Maximus the Confessor writes.[12] Christ is the *Pontifex Maximus,* the greatest of all bridge-builders, who spans the infinite world of God (including the personalized world of the three Persons) and the finite world of mankind and created beings. St. Maximus writes:

> We are astonished to see how the finite and the infinite-things which exclude one another and cannot be mixed—are found to be united in Him and are manifested mutually the one in the other. For the unlimited is limited in an ineffable manner, while the limited is stretched to the measure of the unlimited.[13]

The Second Person as Logos has been revealing the hidden Godhead from the beginning of creation with a personalized act different from the Father. The Father and Source of all being creates all the created world in and through His Word by the overshadowing of His Spirit of love. "Through him all things came to be, not one thing had its being but through him. All that came to be had life in him . . . " (Jn 1:1-2). The Word, within the "con-actual," one, energetic manifestation of God, exerts His own proper, personalistic action. This, Scripture reveals to us as a specific act of imaging the Father through knowledge discovered throughout all nature and within the intellectual powers of man himself.

But through the Incarnation the Second Person continues now through the humanity assumed by the Logos to reveal Himself to us through specific actions reflecting that immanent action of the Son within the Trinity. The human nature of Christ is totally penetrated by the one, divine nature, yet it always remains distinct from that divine nature. It is "existentially" united to the Second Person of the Trinity and not to the First, the Father, nor to the Third, the Holy Spirit.

THEOSIS—DIVINIZATION

St. Athanasius succinctly summarizes the end of the Incarnation:

> The Divine Word was made man that we might become gods. He was made visible through His body in order that we might have an idea of the invisible Father. He has supported the outrages of men in order that we may have a part of His immortality.[14]

As the Heavenly Father eternally begets His Son, so in the "economic" order in history, in the life of Jesus Christ and in a parallel way in our own lives, that same Father is begetting His Son, Jesus Christ, and through Him and His Holy Spirit, He is begetting us in His Son to be His adopted children. St. Cyril of Alexandria writes:

> By the Incarnation we also in Him and through Him according to nature and grace have been made sons of God. According to nature insofar as we are one in Him (through the same human nature); by participation and according to grace through Himself in the Spirit.[15]

The end of our lives is to grow continually into an ever increasing awareness of oneness in Christ Jesus. This is what the Greek Fathers mean by *divinization.* We are to live in the "likeness" of Jesus Christ, that is, to share in His very own life made possible by the Holy Spirit. St. Bernard preached that God entices us to love Him by giving us the humanity of His Son as the point of attraction. Jesus Christ images the divinity of God that radiates through the frailness and lowliness of His humanity. His meekness and gentleness draw us without any threatening fear to surrender to His Spirit. The glory or power of God in His Word radiates in the teachings and miracles and healings of Jesus in Scripture.

It is through this man, Jesus of Nazareth, who will die and be raised up from the dead, that all of God's grace and glory will come to us.

> Indeed, from his fullness we have, all of us, received—
> yes, grace in return for grace,
> since, though the Law was given through Moses,
> grace and truth have come through Jesus Christ.
> No one has ever seen God;
> it is the only Son, who is nearest to the Father's heart,
> who has made him known (Jn 1:16-18).

Jesus Christ perfectly and faithfully represents His Father to us in human communication of words and actions. When He loves us, especially by dying for us on the Cross, we can experience the love of the Father. "As the Father has loved me, so I have loved you" (Jn 15:9). Everything He says or does is *the* Word of God. He can do nothing but what the Father tells Him to do. Yet only Jesus Christ, the Second Person of the Trinity in His human nature, goes to His death. It is not the Father who dies for us nor the Holy Spirit. Yet all three Persons are involved in the Incarnation and Redemption, in our sanctification, each according to His own personalized acts. The Father begets His Son through the overshadowing of the Spirit, as St. Luke records in Lk 1:35. The Father continues acting His personalized role as Begetter in our own divinization through His Son and the Holy Spirit.

THE ROLE OF THE HOLY SPIRIT

The goal of our human existence is to be divinized through the personalized actions of the Father, Son and Holy Spirit into a likeness to the Son of God in the Holy Spirit. It is a process of becoming as God is: a We-community that is personalized Love in a oneness of nature and in uniqueness of persons. As both the Son and the Holy Spirit "proceed" from the Father as from their Source, so they cannot be separated in their "economic" actions that, nevertheless, are distinctive to each Person.

Because the Spirit is "hypostasized" Love binding the Father and Son together, some modern Orthodox theologians like to describe the work of the Holy Spirit in terms of a *kenosis* or emptying, a self-giving, the characteristic of personalized love. St. Paul describes the condescension of God's Word in taking upon Himself the form of a servant and emptying Himself by becoming obedient unto the death of the cross (Ph 2:5-8). That action of Jesus Christ who now is in glory goes on, due to the humanity that links Him with all of us human beings. But the *kenosis* of the Holy Spirit is a constant, hidden giving of the Father and Son to us that persists from Pentecost until the Parousia in this economy of salvation.[16]

The personality of the Holy Spirit is hidden in a personalized *Humility* that characterizes Love itself. He is personified Holiness because He reflects the essence of divine holiness.[17] The holiness of God is seen as triune Love in the Holy Spirit that S. Bulgakov calls: "hypostatic Love."[18]

The Holy Spirit is both the Giver and the Gift of life (Jn 6:63). He gives divine life to us through Jesus Christ but He is also the Father's Gift to us through Jesus Christ. All we have to do is to ask for this Gift and the Father will give us a share in Him (Lk 11:13). Jesus tells us also that Spirit is the "Parakletos" (Jn 16:24), who also gives us righteousness and peace (Rm 14:17). And above all He gives us love that makes it possible for us to be united in filiation with the Father (Jn 15:9; 17:26; Rm 5:5; Rm 8:15, Ga 4:6). The Spirit ushers us into the Kingdom of God. To seek the Kingdom of God is to seek the Holy Spirit for He pours into our hearts all the gifts necessary, not only to enter into living relationship with the Father and Jesus Christ, but also to build up the Kingdom of God.

The personality and work of the Holy Spirit can be seen only in the light of the personality and work of the Father and the Son. The Spirit is present in the eternal birth of the Son. So also He realizes the conception of the Son in history in the womb of Mary. So also the Spirit effects our own being begotten of the Father through the Son. As Jesus in His lifetime was submissive to the Spirit and all of His acts—miracles, healings, forgiving of sins, driving out devils, especially the surrender of His very own life into the hands of His Heavenly Father—were performed by the action of the Spirit within the heart of Jesus Christ, so we find our fullness as human beings by being submissive to the Holy Spirit. The work of Jesus and the Spirit in the Incarnation and Redemption and in Pentecost through the Church of Jesus Christ is climaxed in the goal of the mutual cooperation of Jesus Christ and the Spirit to divinize us into children of the Heavenly Father. Neither Person is more important nor does one do more than the other. They "co-serve" each other to "recapitulate" or bring to completion the Father's eternal plan of creating us and sharing His life through His Son incarnate through the Spirit of Love.

As the Spirit brings the Father and Son together into a loving community and brings about in that mutual love a union of love and a self-knowledge in self-giving to each other, so the same Spirit brings us, many brothers and sisters, into the one begotten Son, Jesus Christ and constitutes the Body of Christ, the Church. Thomas Hopko shows the completing work of the Holy Spirit:

> Just as the work of Christ would be devoid of power without the 'power from on high' in a Pascha without a Pentecost, so would the Way remain unwalkable, the Truth unknowable and the Life unlivable. The Spirit comes to make possible in men all that Christ is by nature by the gracious gift of his presence. This is what St. Maximus means when he says that men are called to be by grace all that Christ is by nature. And what St. Basil means when he announces so boldly that men are 'creatures who have received a command to be god.'[19]

The role of the Spirit is especially "personalized" in our relationships to God as we see that He is not only the hidden person that is in the intimate relationships between Father and Son, but He also is the one who brings to the Father and the Son their unique knowledge and love of themselves and of each other precisely as persons. We come into our unique identity as persons, loved infinitely by the Father and His Son, Jesus, through the working of the Spirit that indwells us as in a temple (1 Co 3:16). We do not know how to pray, but the Spirit comes to our rescue and the Father knows what He is saying within us (Rm 8:26-27).

The greatest work of the Spirit is to unite us with God and as we are united with Him, especially in the personalistic relationships of the three Persons, we are capable of exercising His gifts, particularly the greatest, the gift of love and entering into a unity in the Body of Christ. Such a sense of oneness between ourselves and God and at the same time with every other living creature is the work of the Holy Spirit who infuses into us the gift of contemplation where prayer becomes love. Teilhard de Chardin beautifully expresses this:

> Reality is charged with a divine Presence. As the mystics sense and portray it, everything becomes physically and literally lovable in God; and reciprocally God becomes knowable and lovable in all that surrounds us. In the greatness and depths of its cosmic stuff in the maddening number of elements and events which compose it, and in the fullness of the general currents which dominate and set it in motion like a great wave, the World, filled with God, no longer appears to our opened eyes as anything but a milieu and an object of universal communion.[20]

GOD IN ALL

Such a contemplative person lives in the dynamic, creative presence of God in all things. He may start with a sunset or a small flower. He finds that God is there totally. He no longer feels the need to run frantically throughout the wonders of this world or to exhaust the gamut of human experiences in order to find God. This was perhaps more necessary in the beginning of his prayer life. As persons become more and more advanced in contemplation, especially by the loving presence of the Holy Spirit unifying all things in Christ who leads us to the Heavenly Father, they easily intuit God in all things. Touching anything created yields to them the loving presence of God at the core of all reality.

The dichotomy between the sacred and the secular worlds breaks down as does the separation between work and prayer. Whatever such a person is doing, he finds the Divine Presence everywhere in the unity of all things and this forces him out of himself in a spirit of worship and service. We are touching here ultimately the essential in celibacy. It is not so much physical, although in some chosen callings it includes this witness also. But theologically as experienced celibacy, it is the gift of the Holy Spirit to one who is now totally open to the presence of God and in love with the whole world because he has already participated in an experience of "seeing" God in all things and all things in God. Such a person cannot for a moment love another human being for himself alone. Yet he does not love that person only as a *means* to God. His love is a total grasp of the unique person and the unique presence of God that yields at the same time the unique presence of the personalized acts constituting each Divine Person as Father, Son and Holy Spirit.

We learn to experience God at the heart of all matter.[21] We love each being, this thing, this person, this tree, and God at the same time. We no longer have to move from this to God but we see at one and the same time the created being and the infinite love of God who creates this being and gives it to us as a gift of His love. We find the gift and the Giver in the same look.

Julian of Norwich expresses this well in her pondering of God in a little thing no bigger than a hazelnut that she holds in her hand.

I looked at it with the eye of my understanding and thought: What can this be? I was amazed that it could last, for I thought that because of its littleness it would suddenly have fallen into nothing. And I was answered in my understanding: It lasts and always will, because God loves it; and thus everything has being through the love of God . . . It is that God is the Creator and the protector and the lover. For until I am substantially united to him, I can never have perfect rest or true happiness, until, that is, I am so attached to him that there can be no created thing between my God and me.[22]

GOD WITHIN US

The progress in contemplation is to move more intimately toward God as the core of all reality, but this core is a bundle of infinite, unconfining Love. And as we grow in greater union with God, we begin to live in the power of that burning love that surrounds us in all things and permeates the depths of our being. Prayer moves away from a *doing*, above all, a speaking to God as to an object, to become a constant state of *being* in His love.

When Jesus spoke about prayer He used in His native Aramaic language the word *zlotha*, coming from the root word *zla*, as Dr. Rocco A. Errico explains.[23] This word means literally to "set a trap." In its modern use it would refer to focus in, to tune in to another's communication. Prayer for Jesus was adjusting His whole being to the presence of God living within His humanity. It was surrendering in His human consciousness to the trinitarian God, the Father, Son and Holy Spirit, living within Him and all about Him. Prayer was for Jesus to be receptive to God's personalized love actions at every moment. He surrendered to that love and became Godly-love toward all who met Him.

As Jesus grew in wisdom and knowledge and grace before God and men (Lk 2:52), He entered into a fuller awareness of God's perfect love and self-giving. For us contemplation is a growth through the infusion of faith, hope and love by the Spirit of Jesus Christ in awareness that God is always present loving us intimately and infinitely. How our attitude toward prayer changes when we see it as a listening and a receiving of God's communicating love for us, always constant, never changing!

God cannot increase His love for us, for in Christ Jesus has He not given us the fullness of His love? Can the indwelling Trinity be only imperfectly present in you? Does God wait for you to tell Him that you love Him and then He will come to you with a greater love? Does God's love for us become more ardent and perfect after we have performed for Him some good work? No, prayer is not our attempt to change God so that He will love us more. It is our "tuning in" to God's all-pervasive presence as perfect love. It is to find Him in all things as the power that creates and sustains creatures in being (Ac 17:28).

Above all, it is to live interiorly in the light of the trinitarian indwelling within us. We have seen that this "good news" of the triune God living within us can come to us only through God's revelation, known in Holy Scripture and in the Church that has received the knowledge and understanding to teach us prophetically with the mind of God. Through the mysteries of the Incarnation, death and resurrection of the Word-made-flesh, and His giving to us a constant release of the Spirit of love, we can believe with certainty that, as we die to sin or self-love, we open ourselves up more and more to the eternal, trinitarian community of love within us and around us.

As we die to our self-absorption and open to God's loving presence within us, God's gift of contemplation brings us a new way of knowing God and of receiving His eternal love for one another. Louis de Blois expresses this new level of living in God's indwelling love:

> The soul, having entered the vast solitude of the Godhead, happily loses itself; and enlightened by the brightness of most lucid darkness, becomes through knowledge as if without knowledge, and dwells in a sort of wise ignorance. And although it knows not what God is, to whom it is united by pure charity, although it sees not God as He is in His glory, it yet learns by experience that He infinitely transcends all sensible things, and all that can be apprehended by the human intellect concerning Him. It knows God by this intimate embrace and contact better than the eyes of the body know the visible sun. This soul well knows what true contemplation is.[24]

GOD WITHIN AND WITHOUT

This loving God truly invades us, no longer as an idea or a thought, but as the Source of all life. He drives out of our hearts all vestige of sin and darkness and transforms us into His loving light. As we get caught up inside of God's invading energies of love, we find ourselves gradually being consumed by the Trinity's mutual love for each other and for us. We become a prism by which God can radiate

His love to all that we touch. We become a magnifying
glass, to use the example of the Gorlitz shoemaker and
mystic, Jacob Boehme (+1624), that allows the rays of
God's warm love to burst into flame and to enflame the
world with godly love.

As we experience the transforming love of the triune
God, we surrender more completely each day to be mould-
ed by the interior action of the Trinity. Our filial abandonment to the operations of the Trinity is at once also a
movement outwardly towards the world. From an
anonymous world-community we move interiorly to meet
the loving and personalized *We* community of Father, Son
and Holy Spirit. The completion of that inner movement is
an outward thrust back to the world community to be a
servant through whom God can actualize a world community of *I, Thou* and *We,* that is the Body of Christ, the
Church, ever conscious of being the Bride of Christ.

The degree of God's invasion of us, or rather of how
much we surrender to allow His all-invading presence to
transform us, is measured infallibly by the testimony of the
fruit of the Holy Spirit produced in us as we relate toward
other creatures (GA 5:22). Love, peace, joy, gentleness,
kindliness, patience and forbearance are the result of our
awareness that the Heavenly Father holds us in His two
hands, Jesus Christ and His Spirit, and that He loves us,
infinitely. We show the presence and influence of the
indwelling Trinity by the simple faith we have in the
goodness of others who also are "invaded" by God. We
trust others because we have let go of the control over our
own lives in our surrender to God's interior guidance.

Compassionate mercy moves us, as it did Jesus, to
bind up the wounds and to embrace the homeless of this
world. The love of God in us gives us a share in God's love

which is "always patient and kind; it is never jealous; love is never boastful or conceited; it is never rude or selfish . . . it is always ready to excuse, to trust, to hope, and to endure whatever comes" (1 Co 13:4-7).

This cannot be done except by embracing the cross of self-denial and emptying ourselves, as Jesus did. It is to live fully our Baptism by dying to our self-containment to rise in the newness of the trinitarian life within us, to live a life of self-giving to others. It is to experience at every moment the power of God's Spirit who brings us human beings into a unity or communion of loving brothers and sisters of the only begotten Son of God who leads us to the Father of us all.

In a word, to be invaded by God is to allow God to invade the world by our being present to God who is everywhere present as loving, personalized energies. It is to become so emptied of our nothingness and sinfulness that the Trinity may pour out its richness of life upon the whole world. It is not only to find the Trinity living within us, but it is to make the world around us present to that same immanently present and loving Trinity.

The words of Teilhard de Chardin suggest a proper conclusion to this chapter:

Seeing the mystic immobile, crucified or rapt in prayer, some may perhaps think that his activity is in abeyance or has left this earth: they are mistaken. Nothing in the world is more intensely alive and active than purity and prayer, which hang like an unmoving light between the universe and God. Through their serene transparency flow the waves of creative power, charged with natural virtue and with grace. What else but this is the Virgin Mary?[25]

6

CHRIST IS IN YOU (Col 1:28)

If other centuries witnessed man's discovery of God in nature, in God's revealed Word among His People or man's discovery of God in the unfolding of human intelligence as shown during the Renaissance and the Industrial Revolution, our 20th century must be characterized as man in search of who he is as person. Experimental and in-depth psychology, psychiatry, psychoanalysis, phenomenology, para-psychology, down to the mind-expanding courses of yoga, Silva mind control, TM, *est,* and transactional analysis and so forth bear witness to modern man's search, no longer outside in nature and in the world of doing, but inside of himself to study his psyche.

Into himself he plunges to undergo the most fascinating journey through inner space. Dangers rear up out of the dark shadows of yester-years' repressed experiences. Shakespeare reminds us that all of us "in his time plays many parts. His acts being seven ages."[1] Carl Jung tells us that:

individuation means becoming a single, homogeneous being, and, in so far as 'individuality' embraces our innermost, last and incomparable uniqueness, it also implies
becoming one's own self. We could therefore translate individuation as 'coming to selfhood' or 'self-realization.'[2]

INDIVIDUATION

This process of individuation demands passing
beyond the superficial levels of our own controlled consciousness in order to pass into the innermost core of our
being. Great discipline is required for this. Silence and
aloneness with the Transcendent Absolute are necessary.
But as one passes through layers of psychic experiences,
danger zones rear up. The voyager into the interior passes
into waters filled with hidden rocks ready to capsize the
small sailing vessel. Repressed material that has been
drowned in the unconscious can rise threateningly to
disturb such a pilgrim into inner space.

Flashes and lights, psychic powers of telepathy, communing with the dead can come forth. What is reality,
what is hallucination before the beckoning visions of entic-
ing forms that whirl over the screen of our consciousness?
Voices that we recognize and strange voices too give their
messages with impelling realism. Again, what is real, what
is false? The rocks of Scylla and Charybdis come close and
we could capsize. Do we withdraw or push deeper?

William B. Yeats describes well how man seeks to
distract himself from such confrontation with his "dread"
self.

The child pursuing lizards in the grass,
The sage, who deep in central nature delves,
The preacher watching for the evil hour to pass,
All these are souls that fly from their dread selves.[3]

Although most of us believe that the superficial "self," what Carl Jung calls the "persona," is our true self, there lies even beyond this, reached through the long process called "individuation," our true Self. We need to live in paradox and antinomy. This we fear for we like security where everything is clear, daylight, distinct and we are in complete control. We must choose, if we are to find our true Self, in the words of Yeats, not

> . . . . to destroy
> All those antinomies
> Of day and night . . . .[4]

We must be ready to push beyond the illusion of unity in our superficial "self" to seek an integration of personality or of wholeness of person that needs the healing power of the Absolute. Hermann Hesse puts it in his *Steppenwolf* that, though it appears to be an inborn and imperative need of all men to regard the superficial self as a true unity, yet daring men of genius "break through the illusion of the unity of the personality and perceive that the self is made up of a bundle of selves . . . "[5] It is the search for that true Self which lies beyond the "bundle of selves" that prayerful encounter with God as love is all about.

JESUS, THE WAY TO OUR TRUE SELF

Christianity reveals clearly what an honest examination of our own human lives would reveal, namely, that as St. Paul says, there is sin in our members (Rm 7:20). We cannot effect our own integration without the power of the Divine Physician, the Master Psychiatrist, Jesus Christ. He has the fullness of life in Himself, the true Image of the Invisible God.

Scheeben aptly expresses this sublime teaching in these words:

Since the Holy Spirit proceeds from the love of the Father for the Son, and through the Son is to be poured out over the whole world, nothing is more appropriate than that the Son in His humanity, as the head of all creatures, should represent and effect this outpouring of the Holy Spirit in the outpouring of His blood, and that this latter outpouring should become the real sacrament of the other outpouring. Is not the shedding of the blood of Christ's heart the truest pledge that He and His Father will, in their own Spirit, share with us the innermost character, so to speak, of their divinity? Is not the blood with its purifying, warming, life-giving energy the sacrament of the corresponding activities of the Holy Spirit? And is not the mystical body and corporal bride of the God-man formed from the blood of Christ's heart by the power of the Holy Spirit dwelling in Him, just as the Spirit of the Father and the Son and their partner in love springs forth from their divine heart.[6]

It is only through the Holy Spirit that we can know the full Jesus Christ and our true selves in loving oneness with Him. "We know that he lives in us by the Spirit that he has given us" (1 Jn 3:24). The work of the Spirit is to make us holy or sanctified as we live more consistently, not only as Jesus lived in complete submission in all things to His Father, but above all *with* Jesus living in us. Our "individuation" into the fully integrated human being you and I should be by God's unique love for each of us can be realized only by the interacting, loving relationships of the Father, Son and Holy Spirit.

This chapter deals with the indwelling presence of Jesus Christ within us. But it is pre-supposed that we keep in mind the inseparability of the Son and the Father. The Holy Spirit is also always present, uniting them into their loving oneness and uniqueness.

TOO GOOD TO BELIEVE

There are many truths in Christianity to which we give lip service or a head-knowledge consent, yet if we were to live by them, such revealed truths would change our lives. One such truth is that a Christian in the state of grace possesses the risen, glorified Jesus Christ. By living constantly our Baptism of dying to self, the words of St. Paul apply to us: ". . . you have died and now the life you have is hidden with Christ in God" (Col 3:3). St. Paul continuously speaks of the Christian who must put on Jesus Christ (Ga 3:27; Ep 4:24) and live *in* Christ.

The Greek preposition has a sense of movement and can also mean *into* Christ. It is an engrafting on to Christ (Rm 6:5; Jn 15:1-8). Such an "incorporation" into Christ means that the Spirit quickens us, as we freely consent to lose our false identity, maintained through self-love, fear, aggressive attack against others, to realize that the Risen Christ is dynamically alive within us. "I have been crucified with Christ, and I live now not with my own life but with the life of Christ who lives in me" (Ga 2:19-20).

St. Maximus the Confessor well describes this great mystery of the indwelling Christ:

> The Word of God, born once in the flesh (such is His kindness and His goodness), is always willing to be born spiritually in those who desire Him. In them He is born as an infant as He fashions Himself in them by means of their virtues. He reveals Himself to the extent that He knows someone is capable of receiving Him. He diminishes the revelation of His glory not out of selfishness but because He recognizes the capacity and resources of those who desire to see Him. Yet, in the transcendence of mystery, He always remains invisible to all.[7]

MAN'S DIGNITY

This is the incomparably "Good News": Jesus Christ lives within us. We are, in the words of St. Ignatius of Antioch (+115), *Christ-bearers (Christophoroi).* The Kingdom of God is truly within us. What amazing love God has for us in that He gave us His only-begotten Son (Jn 3:16) who in the flesh was able to die for love of us and to image the infinite love that the Father has for each one of us, but through that death the Father *glorified* Him (Ph 2:9).

In His risen existence the full Jesus Christ, God-Man, can now be *in us* and we, by His Holy Spirit, can be *in Him.* This is God's greatest gift, the Spirit unseparated from the risen Christ. The two personalized relations within the Trinity are communicated to the Christian. This gift contains both Jesus Christ and the Holy Spirit who have their full being in relationship to the Father.

St. Paul must have been carried away many times as he understood that this Jesus Christ, who died for him out of a personal love (Ga 2:20), also lived within him. He calls it "the mystery of Christ" (Ep 3:4). This knowledge was given him as a gift of faith and he burns to communicate a share in that faith-revelation to all he meets. He wishes to be a Jew to the Jew, weak to the weak, to win all to Christ (1 Co 9:20-22). St. Paul has accepted the loss of everything for this indwelling Christ. Everything else is considered as rubbish as long as he can have Christ (Ph 3:9). His one prayer is:

All I want is to know Christ and the power of his resurrection and to share his sufferings by reproducing the pattern of his death (Ph 3:10).

Psalm 8 describes what could most perfectly be applied to the Christian in whom Christ dwells:

Ah, what is man that you should spare a thought for him,
the son of man that you should care for him? Yet you have
made him little less than a god, you have crowned him with
glory and splendour . . . .(Ps 8:4-5).

We, of all God's creatures, have been made according to His very own image and likeness that is Jesus Christ. Only we have been gratuitously given the great grace of receiving the lavished love of the Father through His gift of His Son Jesus and the Spirit whereby we are really His children (1 Jn 3:1-2; Rm 8:15; Ga 4:6). We have been transformed into new creatures, into a new creation since we are "in Christ" (2 Co 5:17). We actually have been called to become participators in the divine nature (2 P 1:4). Jesus Christ with the Father abides in us (Jn 14:23). We belong to Him. His divine life courses through our entire being because we are as a branch is to the vine in our intimate, living relationships with Jesus Christ.

St. Symeon powerfully captures the vision in which Christian mystics live who grow daily in the awareness of their inter-penetration with the living, indwelling Christ:

I thank you that You, even when I was sitting in
  darkness,
revealed Yourself to me, You enlightened me,
You granted me to see the light of Your countenance
  that is unbearable to all.
I remained seated in the middle of the darkness, I know,
but, while I was there, surrounded by darkness,
You appeared as light, illuminating me completely from
  Your total light.

And I became light in the night,
I who was found in the midst of darkness.
Neither the darkness extinguished Your light completely,
nor did the light dissipate the visible darkness,
but they were together, yet completely separate,
without confusion, far from each other,
surely not at all mixed,
except in the same spot where they filled everything . . .
So I am in the darkness,
yet still I am in the middle of the light.
How can darkness receive within itself a light
and, without being dissipated by the light,
it still remains in the middle of the light?
O awesome wonder which I see doubly,
with my two sets of eyes, of the body and of the soul!
Listen now; I am telling you the awesome mysteries
of a double God who came to me as to a double man.
He took upon Himself my flesh and He gave me His Spirit.
and I became also god by divine grace,
a son of God but by adoption
O what dignity, what glory![8]

Our dignity by grace—God as uncreated energies of love elevating us by a created relationship that we can call sanctifying grace—is to be in union with Jesus Christ by His Spirit so that the Heavenly Father looks upon us and loves us as only one Son, Jesus Christ. This is the mystery hidden for centuries, as St. Paul writes, that has now been revealed to his saints.

It was God's purpose to reveal it to them and to show all the rich glory of this mystery to pagans. The mystery is Christ among you, your hope of glory. This is the Christ we proclaim, this is the wisdom in which we thoroughly train everyone and instruct everyone, to make them all perfect in Christ (Col 1:27-28).

LIVES HOLY AND PLEASING TO GOD

Christ within us is light that dissipates the darkness. To be a Christian is to become ever more aware that Christ lives in us. It is to live in a oneness with Him. It is to receive His constant love that showed itself on the cross but that was captured forever in the risen Christ. If there is the darkness of sin within us, our Christianity must be occupied with the dissipation of such darkness. Sin in any form is the absence of the life of Christ in our lives.

Our Christian life, therefore, comprises a struggle against sin. But our Christian life is not exclusively the struggle. The negative elements must be done away with in order that the positive focus of true Christianity can be accentuated. And this means to live in the reality that the risen Christ lives within us through His Spirit. We truly are now part of God's family insofar as we exist totally in Christ.

The Christian life is very positive. It is a growth into the fullness of Christ. It entails great inner discipline in order that Christ be the norm of all of our thoughts, words and deeds. "Every thought is our prisoner, captured to be brought into obedience to Christ. Once you have given your complete obedience, we are prepared to punish any disobedience" (2 Co 10:5-6).

To put on Christ and to live in Him at every moment is to experience deeply at all times the indwelling presence of the risen Lord. But such an experience is a transforming action between the resurrected Christ and ourselves. Within us the indwelling Christ abides with the Father. His primary work is to release *within us* the Spirit of love who alone can illumine our minds and ignite our hearts to realize constantly the infinite love that Christ and His Father have for us.

Sin is destroyed not so much by our own efforts but by the gift of the Spirit who permeates us with a new, divine life within us that orientates all things to the Father in union with Jesus Christ. By the Holy Spirit we are transformed into genuine children of God and we grow into that divine filiation by His infusion of greater faith, hope and love (Rm 8:15; Ga 4:6). We live an intimate relationship with Jesus so that His name is not only on our lips and in our hearts, but we are given the gift to contemplate ourselves living each moment in His risen life present within us.

Now this Lord is the Spirit, and where the Spirit of the Lord is, there is freedom. And we, with our unveiled faces reflecting like mirrors the brightness of the Lord, all grow brighter and brighter as we are turned into the image that we reflect; this is the work of the Lord who is Spirit (2 Co 3:18).

This is the "delectatio victrix" of St. Augustine, the conquering sweetness that makes it easy for us to give up all lesser attachments to ourselves, to others or to things in order to "be in Christ." As we grow in awareness of how intimately Christ dwells within us and of how perfect is His love for us, then any sacrifice to uproot whatever may pose as a threat to this loving union will be made promptly and joyfully.

But more importantly, such a Christian will seek to return love for love received. A life of going outward toward a world community and giving of oneself flows from an identity of being nobly loved by God in His Son, Jesus Christ, through His Spirit. Experiencing our oneness with Jesus Christ, we can go out in that union to live according to His mind. We move away from imperatives and commands to embrace the true freedom of children of God who strive always to act according to their true dignity as children of God. This is the truth according to which God has created us. When we seek to live each moment with such motivation, true freedom results, bringing us deep peace and joy.

This awareness becomes progressively an infusion into our minds and hearts by the Holy Spirit. But in the beginning stages of "being in Christ," it is necessary during the day to reflect on how a person in Christ would act in all his thoughts, words and deeds. Jacques Leclercq writes:

> The inner life constitutes an indispensable and essential means. In order to unify our life in God, we must direct our thinking, realize what God is, just how all value in general and in particular is related to Him. We shall never set our life in order unless we have clear and habitual consciousness, as actual as possible, of the way in which each of our acts is related to the general task of reduction to the One which we must achieve . . . Action can only be well ordered if we fix our mind on the One to start with. This is achieved in recollection only if our consciousness of the One has become sufficiently deep for us to be able to refer to it spontaneously whenever we are called to act.[9]

But as we are faithful in our desire to let Christ rule us, He takes over more completely in our lives and we then do less. Our doing becomes an active receptivity to Christ's indwelling presence. "Be it done unto me according to Thy Word" (Lk 1:38). We are *in Christ* as in our home. There is an ease and a familiarity. We know the feeling when we have travelled for a long time away from home and enter again into our familiar home. We should over the years have an ability to be at home with Christ. At each moment we are to enter "into" Christ, to put on His mind in loving submission and then, through the intuitive discernment of the Holy Spirit, we are to act.

TRUE LOVE IS OBEDIENCE

Obedience to Christ is the index of our love for Him and of our union with Him. Such loving submission demands the free sacrifice of our own wills, in the sense of our autonomous, "carnal" and compulsive wills that we close off from the illumination of Christ's Spirit.

Love of Christ and union with Him is impossible without obedience on our part which unites our will with that of Christ. This is a freely chosen, spontaneous act that is done sheerly out of love and not fear or coercion. Thus we can see that the indwelling of Christ within us brings about an intimate union of our wills with that of Christ which union of wills expresses itself in the way of life lived in love.

To remain in Christ is intimately associated with keeping His commandments in a spirit of love (Jn 15:10; 1 Jn 4:12, 16) and with bearing much fruit (Jn 15:10). Thus union with Christ and living in His love according to His mind are essential characteristics of all Christians and not a level of perfection to be attained by a few chosen persons.

IF YOU KEEP MY WORD

While reading the Fathers of the desert, I have often been impressed by the fact that the one work they assigned to all Christians, regardless of their state of life, is to observe Christ's commandments. We hear from Christ Himself that, if we truly love Him, we will keep His word "and my Father will love him, and we shall come to him and make our home with him" (Jn 14:23). Keeping Christ's word, for such athletes of the desert, was more than observing the ten commandments. It was more than observing all that Jesus commanded as found in the New Testament.

It came down to a state of listening to the indwelling Christ as He, through His Spirit, revealed to the Christian the mind of the Father in each event. Often such spiritual writers of the Christian East employed the symbol of seeing Christ within themselves as light, illuminating their minds as to the will of God.

The end of the Incarnation is precisely that God's divine life may be restored within our inner being by Jesus Christ entering within our spiritual faculties by grace. We should desire hungrily to possess this inner presence of Jesus Christ as light in a more conscious, unifying way. As we grow in deeper silencing of our "heart" and begin to see how bound we are by shadow and darkness, by sense pleasures and false values, in such a state of alienation, we cry continually to see more of Christ's light, to experience more and more His assimilating presence that will bridge the abyss separating our sinful selves from Him in a union of loving surrender. Jesus Christ, the Light of the world, makes Himself "seen within us."

THE LIGHT WITHIN

No one can reach this level of "seeing Jesus Christ within." No spiritual director can teach another how to reach this state of being in the "light of Christ." Only God can reveal it to us in experience. And the first step to such an abiding in the light of Christ that dwells within us is to realize by ardent faith that He does truly live within us. This we have seen revealed so often in the New Testament. A beautiful description of Jesus Christ, the Risen Lord, indwelling within the Christian, is given by a 13th century monk:

> In me, in my most interior Jesus is present. All outside of our heart is only to discover the treasure hidden interiorly in the heart. There is found that sepulcher of Easter and there the new life. 'Woman, why do you weep? Whom do you seek? Whom you seek, you already possess and you do not know Him? You have the true, eternal joy and still you weep? It is more intimate to your being and still you seek it outside! You are there, outside, weeping near the tomb. Your heart is my tomb. And I am not there dead, but I repose there, living always. Your soul is My garden. You are right when you believed that I was the gardener. I am the New Adam. I work and supervise My paradise. Your tears, your love, your desire, all this is My work. You possess Me at the most intimate level of your being, without knowing it and this is why you seek Me outside. It is then outside also that I appeared to you and also that I make you to return to yourself, to make you find at the intimacy of your being Him whom you seek outside.[10]

Jesus often referred to Himself as light, especially in St. John's Gospel. "I, the light, have come into the world, so that whoever believes in me need not stay in the dark any more" (Jn 12:46). Our growth in perfection consists in the intensity of union that we attain through the conscious awareness of Jesus Christ living in us with the resulting surrender totally of ourselves in a perfect *symbiosis* of two wills operating as one through the union brought about by the Holy Spirit.

Jesus Christ lives within us baptized Christians. And yet we know that there is also much darkness of selfishness living within as well. The life of Christ within us grows as we yield to His real presence within us, as we co-operate

with Him in all of our thoughts and actions. Since St.
Thomas Aquinas, theologians in the West have been extremely preoccupied with the problem of how we human
beings can relate to the indwelling Divine Persons. What
kind of grace brings about the created relationship, for example, between ourselves and God the Father or God the
Son or God the Holy Spirit?[11] This will always remain a
mystery and before the real experience any man-made ex-
planation is as the "straw" by which St. Thomas Aquinas
compared his own theological writings when he compared
them to the mystical experience as he knelt before the
Crucifix.

If we remain with Holy Scripture and hold on firmly
to the fact that Jesus Christ truly abides within the
dynamically alive Christian, and that He is "seen" in some
contemplative way as light, we perhaps will be able to go
farther in at least experiencing the presence of Jesus
Christ. Jesus Christ tells us that He lives in us and He is
light. His light or personalized presence shines day and
night within our hearts and in our intelligence. It bathes us
in His radiance and knows no setting. It draws us into the
same life-giving and transforming light, "light from
light." This manner of speaking, at least among the
Eastern Fathers, that Christ is light is to say that He is
sensed as present and acting in a loving, transforming manner. It is not in a sensible way as seen with our physical
eyes, but we become aware of Him in an intelligible manner through contemplation.

St. Symeon the New Theologian summarizes well the
consistent teaching of the Greek Fathers on the indwelling
of Christ within the Christian as light:

O stupendous prodigy, of an incomprehensible God, who
works and yet is mysteriously incomprehensible! A man
bears consciously in himself God as light, Him who has

produced and created all things, holding even the man who carries Him. Man carries Him interiorly as a treasure which transcends words, written or spoken, any quality, quantity, image matter and figure, shaped in an inexplicable beauty, all entirely simple as *light,* He who transcends all light.

PRAY ALWAYS

Christian prayer through the faith infused into the one praying by the spirit of Jesus Christ is an on-going process of discovering not only the abyss that separates the Absolute, all-holy God from us sinners, but also the depths of union that exist between us and God in the very depths of our being. Growth in prayer is, therefore, a growth in awareness of God, especially as He lives and acts through His infinite love.

We ought soberly to have an attentive mind, waiting expectantly on God until He comes and visits the soul by means of all of its openings and its paths and senses . . . If, then, you believe these things to be true, as indeed they are, look to yourself to see whether your soul has found its guiding light and the genuine meat and drink which is the Lord. If you have not, seek night and day in order to receive. When, therefore, you see the sun, seek the true Sun. For you are blind. When you gaze on a light, look into your soul to see whether you have found the true and good Light. For all the visible things of the senses are but a shadow of the true realities of the soul.

For there is another man beyond the sensible that is within. And there are other eyes within that Satan has blinded and ears which he has rendered deaf. And Jesus has come to make this inner man healthy.[14]

THE JESUS PRAYER

Such Christians, following the teaching of Pseudo-Macarius and the prayer of the heart, strove to enter within their consciousness ("heart" is the scriptural image used to describe this) and there they found Christ dwelling within. They cried out night and day that the Bridegroom come to them, even though they knew He already possessed them as His bride. Calling upon His name in the same belief of St. Peter, that "this is the only name by which we can be saved" (Ac 4:12), they synchronized their breath with the name of Jesus Christ as their Savior.

To such unsophisticated Christians, God's *Anawim* of the desert, the Spirit of the Risen Christ revealed the essence of the Jesus-event in a living experience. These were the true charismatic Christians, baptized in the Spirit daily by Jesus Christ. They learned to die to all self-centeredness as they experienced the resurrectional power of the presence of Jesus Christ living within them.

The name of Jesus Christ for us modern Christians is also more than a mere recall of our Lord who once lived on this earth and performed healings and miracles and died for love of us. Allowing His name to be present not only on our lips but in our heart (pushing ourselves to be consciously present to Him), we can experience by the Spirit's gifts of deeper infusion of faith, hope and love the presence of Jesus Christ.

Jesus becomes more and more present to us, leading us into the presence of the Father through His Spirit of love. We experience with Mary the growth of Jesus within our hearts. We experience also the Heavenly Father begetting Him and us together in a new birth of His only begotten Son. We experience the Holy Spirit pouring out His gifts that allow us to build up the body of Christ through contemplation and action.

A TRANSFIGURING LIGHT

Above all, as we are bathed in the transfiguring power of the indwelling Jesus, we are able to release the same transfiguring presence of Jesus in the world in which we are present. He "fills the whole creation" (Ep 1:23). Sharing in His priesthood, we can release the Risen Lord and ask Him to transform each person we meet, each material thing we touch, to bring God's Kingdom into being "on earth as it is in Heaven."

What a power a Christian contemplative has to call forth the transforming power of Jesus Christ into his modern world, one that groans so loudly in agony until the full Christ has been born. Such a Christian lives in a paschal hope that although alone he is complete weakness, with Jesus Christ within him he can do all things in Him who strengthens him.

We cry out at all times that the Body of Christ, the total Christ, will be fashioned out of all the material elements that pass through our lives. "Come, Lord Jesus, *Marana tha!*" (Rv 22:20).

FIERY PRAYER

Although Jesus Christ, the Father and the Holy Spirit dwell within us perfectly and completely in an infinite love toward us, yet as we yearn ardently in moments of restful contemplation or in busy work during the day to become more united with God through Christ in His Spirit, our prayer ignites into a longing for God that nothing created

can ever satisfy. St. Isaac of Nineveh describes such contemplative prayer:

> Your heart is aflame, burns like fire day and night; and so
> the whole world seems to you like dust and dung; you even
> have no desire for food, for the sweetness of new flaming
> thoughts, constantly arising in your soul. Suddenly foun-
> tains of tears open up in you, flowing freely like an inex-
> haustible stream and mingling with all your activities, with
> your reading, your prayer or meditation, your eating or
> drinking or aught else. When you see this in your soul, be
> of good cheer, for you have crossed the sea. Then be
> diligent in your work, stand watchfully on guard, that
> grace may increase in you from day to day.[15]

This advanced state of contemplation, resulting from
the awareness of the individual's mystical union with the
Bridegroom, Jesus Christ, burns out any attachment to
oneself or to other creatures. Jesus Christ is all. Such a
contemplative understands what St. Paul meant when he
wrote: "There is only Christ, he is everything and he is in
everything" (Col 3:11).

St. John of the Cross gives a fitting description in his
commentary on *The Living Flame of Love:*

> O living flame of love that with your ardor tenderly
> touches me. Since this flame is a flame of divine life, it
> wounds the soul with the tenderness of God's life, and it
> wounds and stirs it so deeply as to make it dissolve in love.
> What the bride affirmed in the Canticle is fulfilled in the
> soul. She was so moved that her soul melted, and thus she
> says: As soon as He spoke my soul melted (Sg 5:6). For
> God's speech is the effect He produces in the soul.[16]

RETURNING TO THE MARKET PLACE

Having plunged deeply into himself, the Christian contemplative has become transformed into Christ. It is not an absorption or assimilation of the human personhood into Christ. It is the peak of divine love that has brought the human person to a realization of the end for which he was created: to be in the likeness of Jesus Christ. This floods the contemplative with deep repose and interior joy. He senses an inner harmony of having arrived at fulfillment.

And yet the Christian experiences God's unique love poured out also upon every creature. The Christ in him sends him forth to be a mediator to the world. The contemplative has received God's Word. Like the Prophets of old, he is driven out to share that Word with the world. He knows from Holy Scripture that real love of God is tied to genuine, active love of neighbor. But he knows it now by an inner knowledge of oneness with Christ within himself and oneness with the whole Christ outside himself. As God is "toward" him in self-giving through Jesus Christ in His Spirit, so he now intuits both the ideal oneness between himself and all men and women in Christ. But he also intuits the estrangement of so many from that oneness.

He suffers the suffering of Christ to bring the lost sheep into the one fold. He burns with the love of Christ in him that urges him to spend his energies in loving service to others. The silent listening to the indwelling Christ awakens a deeper sense of unconsciousness of the divine intelligence. He experiences easily a greater good and inner meaning and relationship of all things in himself and around him in all creatures being rooted ultimately in God as the Ground of their being.

Through such inner listening to the unfolding of God's Word within himself, he will learn how to respond in harmony with God's promptings. Such praying in the heart brings about an inner tension that can never be done away with. He is at one with God in peace and tranquility and yet he sees not only within himself but above all around him in his daily world the non-reality of what is not yet in Him. The darkness and demonic forces rise from within and from without, urging him to do battle.

In proportion to the transforming power of Christ that he has felt within his "heart," to that degree he can live and work in his world, according to his talents and charisms, in hope of what can be through the resurrectional power of Jesus Christ and His Holy Spirit. He works not only to make the joy of each person he serves to be complete (Jn 1:4), but to make the joy of Jesus Christ and His Father fulfilled.

AUTHENTIC TEST

The power of true Christianity lies in holding out to all of us an active participation in the inner life and love of the triune God. Its teaching on man and what constitutes his true personhood centers around man's ever growing awareness that God has created all things in Jesus Christ. We reach our true identity to the degree that we live *in* Christ, that He and we form a oneness in love.

We need never be in doubt as to how intense this union between Christ and ourselves is. It is measured by our surrender to the indwelling Christ who directs us outwardly to be His "Ambassadors" and "reconcilers" with

Him of the whole world (2 Co 5:18-19). We know the abiding power of Christ loving within us by the love that we show forth to others.

If we love one another, God dwells in us and His love is perfected in us . .. and we have known and believed the love that God has for us. God is love; and he that dwells in love dwells in God and God in him (1 Jn 4:12,16).

With St. Paul we can say that "the love of Christ overwhelms us" (2 Co 5:14). It is the love-energy of Christ operating in us in all of our human relationships. The same Christ that imaged the love of the Heavenly Father by dying for us and for the whole world lives within us. As we yield to His loving, transforming presence, one with Him, the gentle, meek, suffering Servant of Yahweh, we move with Him to serve the world in order to bring it into His very own Body to the glory of the Trinity. Love toward others and humble service determine the intensity of our union with Jesus Christ. Our unity as persons is likewise measured by love and service in humility. These are the signs that we are not only vibrant Christians but fully realized human beings, made according to the image and likeness of Jesus Christ.

7

The Indwelling Holy Spirit

I became an "aficionado" of *Star Trek* the first time I saw that TV program. It was a story of earth men, led by Mr. Spock and Admiral Kirk, on a flight to recover another earth man who had earlier been marooned on a far-away planet. There he had met an intelligent force that would come to him as a whirlwind and suck him inside the wind where in peace and silence the Great Force would communicate with the earth man.

For Christians such a Great Force surrounds us at all times. God covers us with a similar wind, His Holy Spirit, and at deep center we are able to communicate with the triune family of Father, Son and Holy Spirit. This Uncreated Energy of Love is the one God in three relationships, one divine nature, that not only surrounds us and all creatures as God by His essence and power, but brings into being and sustains all of us in our being and, in a very unique way, dwells in us human beings.

By this indwelling presence God communicates Himself to us in knowledge and love. The truth about the communicating presence of God by indwelling within the divinized Christians is solidly attested to in the Gospels and especially in the Epistles of St. Paul. It is sad that so many

Christians give some sort of intellectual assent to this revealed truth but so few allow it to burst forth into their daily lives. We can pray a great deal to God outside ourselves and study Scripture and theology, but unless God's indwelling presence be recognized in life's situations and the power of God's communicative Word and Spirit of love be experienced, we shall make little progress in true Christian living.

REVELATION OF THE INDWELLING SPIRIT

Jesus Christ died and rose from the dead. He was the expressed Word of the Father. But He would have remained a muted Word in the silence of Calvary if in His "glorification" He would not have sent His Holy Spirit, as He promised His Disciples. But if we were to love Him by keeping His commandments, He promised to give us the Comforter who would *abide* in us.

> If you love me you will keep my commandments.
> I shall ask the Father,
> and he will give you another Advocate
> to be with you for ever,
> that Spirit of truth
> whom the World can never receive
> since it neither sees nor knows him;
> but you know him,
> because he is with you, he is in you (Jn 14:15-17).

The Disciples were not to be sad by the Master's leaving for if Jesus did not go, the great Gift of the Spirit would not be given them (Jn 16:7). But when the Spirit of Truth that proceeds from the Father comes, "He will give testimony of me" (Jn 15:27). This Gift of the Spirit that would abide within the Disciples was not to be given only to them. " . . . because the love of God has been poured into our hearts by the Holy Spirit which has been given us" (Rm 5:5). All of us, argues St. Paul, are no longer "unspiritual" but now spiritual, "since the Spirit of God has made his home in you" (Rm 8:9).

We have all been made children of God through the Holy Spirit that lives in us: "The proof that you are sons is that God has sent the Spirit of his Son into our hearts: the Spirit that cries, 'Abba, Father,' and it is this that makes you a son, you are not a slave any more" (Ga 4:6-7). This Spirit dwells in us and bears witness to our highest faculty of knowing and loving, our spirit, that we really are now God's children: "The Spirit himself and our spirit bear united witness that we are children of God" (Rm 8:16).

It has been pointed out in preceding chapters that it is the whole Trinity, Father, Son and Spirit, that comes and abides in us in a very special manner. St. Paul places the presence of the Spirit not only within the whole Body, the Church of Christ, as he writes in 1 Co 3:16,[1] but he has the Spirit as dwelling in the individual Christian. This indwelling is found in his text: "Your body, you know, is the temple of the Holy Spirit, who is in you since you received him from God" (1 Co 6:19).

A SPECIAL PRESENCE

What shines through such revealed texts from Holy Scripture is that there is a special *presence* of God, the Trinity, within the Christian through the "sending" of the

Holy Spirit of Jesus and the Father. Not only is the Spirit dwelling in the hearts of the Christians but He is there exercising a special role. We know that where one Person of the Trinity is there are the other two Persons. In any action of God outside of the Trinity all three Persons concur in the action since they possess the same nature. Now we see the importance of the Greek Fathers' distinction between the essence of the Godhead that is non-communicable to creatures and His uncreated energies of love that is the entire "essential" God in one nature, communicating Himself to the created world. We see also the importance of Karl Rahner's principle that the "immanent" relationships found within the Trinity between the Persons are also operative in the "economic" relationships.[2]

Therefore, as within the Trinity, so in the order of salvation, only the Son and the Holy Spirit proceed from the Father. Hence, only the Son and Holy Spirit can be "sent" into our world. The Son of God is sent by the Father into this world and He alone assumes humanity. The Spirit that binds the Father and Son together in love also proceeds from that love between the Father and the Son. The Spirit, therefore, has a very special function in our regard that flows out of His unique personhood as the bond of love between the Father and the Son. The entire Trinity has equally loved this world and ourselves in this world, yet the Spirit is sent into our hearts to effect our sanctification. He is the one who is always the loving force, always uniting and differentiating in love.

If Scripture attests to the fact that this Holy Spirit is given to us and performs certain actions, it must mean that He is "sent" in a most personalized way, befitting His personal way of being within the Trinity. He is "present" to

us in a similar way as He is present to the Father and the
Son. As the energies of God operating as one nature are
uncreated and never begin or cease to operate, so in a
similar manner, if the "economic" actions of the Holy
Spirit are linked with the "immanent" action of the same
Spirit within the Trinity, such actions being divine, do not
begin or cease to operate. Being sent by the Father and the
Son, the Holy Spirit does not undergo any change or
separation from the Father or the Son. The change must be
within us who receive Him. This is what is called "created
grace." It is especially by the created grace called *sanctifying grace* that we are changed and enter into a new relationship with the Trinity by becoming truly a child of God
the Father, a brother with Jesus and His Spouse and a temple of the Holy Spirit.

It is imperative that we keep in mind, as "primal
grace," the uncreated energies of God which possess
within the one nature of the triune God the individuated,
personalized relations of the three Persons, Father, Son
and Holy Spirit to us. And these personalized relations,
like the uncreated energies, do not come and go. They are
always present. What comes and goes, what begins, exists
and can be destroyed is our response in knowledge and
love to that presence of the three Persons, operating eternally in accordance with their constitutive personalities.
This is the created relationship that flows from the primal
grace. Why this distinction is so important is that we must
hold from Scripture that God truly communicates *Himself*
to us. His communication is not indirectly through grace,
i.e., a created grace, for then we would not truly be receiving God the Gift but we would be receiving a *thing* called

sanctifying grace. This is a created relationship that can grow, be given, can be withdrawn as a gift, but it flows intrinsically from *the* Gift that is God Himself.

St. .Thomas Aquinas well describes God's presence to us in knowledge and love through the created grace called sanctifying grace:

> Over and above the ordinary and common manner in which God is present in all things, namely, by His essence, His power and His presence, as the cause is present in the effects which are a participation in His goodness, there is another and a special presence which is appropriate to rational nature, a presence by which God is said to be present as that which is known is present to the being who knows, and as that which is loved is present to the being who loves. And because a rational and a loving creature by its operation in knowing and loving is placed in contact with God Himself, for that reason it is said that God by this special manner of presence is not only *in* a rational creature, but also that he *dwells* in it as in His temple. No other effect than sanctifying grace can be the reason why of this new manner of presence of the Divine Person. It is therefore solely by sanctifying grace that the Divine Person is thus sent forth and proceeds temporarily . . . And always, together with grace, one receives also the Holy Spirit Himself, who is thus given and sent.[3]

This important text summarizes well for us how God can be present to us through the created relationship called *sanctifying grace*. But there can be a danger in such a presentation. It could appear as though the Holy Spirit comes to us as a result of such a relationship and is not present always in the uncreated energies of love that are

operative regardless of our cooperation or even knowledge
of them. The Holy Spirit is always operating and is always
being sent by the Father and the Son, this even from the
beginning of time. But when we open ourselves in a conversion away from sinfulness and selfish love to His loving
presence, then there is produced a new relationship that is
capable of growth in greater knowledge and love.

The Holy Spirit is constantly being given to all men if
they would only open up to His loving presence. The beginning and the growth depend upon our response and
cooperation. This relationship (not the Holy Spirit) grows
in us every time we open up in ever conscious cooperation
with the Spirit. Throughout the day, whenever we
cooperate with the actual graces given us to perform virtues, especially that of charity, in seeking to do all for the
greater glory of God, this relationship grows in greater intensity. The Holy Spirit takes over our spiritual faculties
and unites us more intensely with the Trinity in knowledge
of God's loving presence and in love as a response to God's
ever-present love.

If we believe that the Holy Spirit comes as a conse-
quence upon sanctifying grace, we tend to objectivize grace
as a "thing" and the Holy Spirit would be thus present,
not immediately and directly, but in the "thing" called
grace. Representative of such "thingafying" grace and the
presence of the indwelling Trinity is the following statement, found so often in similar books that deal with God's
indwelling presence:

> Scarcely has mortal sin been committed, however, when
> the Divine Guests depart, saying again and again those
> fearful words that rang out from the temple of Jerusalem

when the day of its ruin had come: 'Let us go hence! Let us go hence!' The soul thus abandoned by God and His angels becomes the den of demons and the haunt of those venomous creatures that are none other than its malignant passions.[4]

A SUBSTANTIAL PRESENCE

What we find in the scriptural texts concerning the Holy Spirit's relationships with us Christians is solidly confirmed by the early Fathers. They fought heretics, such as the Arians, Macedonians and the *Pneumatomachoi,* who held that the Holy Spirit was not a Divine Person but was a created gift of God.

The basic arguments of the Fathers universally centered around St. Athanasius' reasoning that if the Holy Spirit effects man's participation in the divine nature, the Spirit cannot be a created being, since He brings about an effect, man's divinization, that is above all creatures.

St. Gregory of Nazianzus rather dramatically but to the point phrases the patristic argument that the Holy Spirit truly effects our divinization and does so because He is truly divine.

I cannot believe that I am saved by one who is my equal. If the Holy Spirit is not God, let him first be made God, and then let him deify me his equal . . . Why do you grudge me a complete regeneration? Why do you make me, who am the temple of the Holy Spirit as of God, the habitation of a creature?[5]

If the Holy Spirit brings us into the likeness of Jesus Christ so as to become truly God's children, He must be,

as the Fathers insist, *substantially* present, i.e., according
to His very being as the *Holy* Spirit who by His substance is
the Sanctifier. He Himself must live in us and communicate to us the divine life. If He merely gives us a created
grace, we are not being *gifted* through the Holy Spirit with
the triune God's very nature. Sanctifying grace can never
exist separated from the Holy Spirit, working in His
substantial presence in an analogous manner to His operations within the Trinity.

This point is extremely important. For if the real
Spirit of Christ and the Father is touching us with His
substantial presence, then we can indeed hope to become
completely regenerated, "born of the Spirit" (Jn 3:6).
We must avoid any unscriptural and unpatristic view that
would hold our justification as children of God to be only
an extrinsic title given to us through the blood of Christ,
without a genuine regeneration and divinization as taught
so universally by all of the early Fathers.

St. Cyril of Alexandria aptly summarizes this universal teaching among the Fathers:

> It is untrue to say that we cannot be one with God except
> by union of will. For above that union there is another
> union more sublime and far superior, which is wrought by
> the communication of the Divinity to man, who, while
> keeping his own nature, is, so to speak, transformed into
> God, just as iron plunged into fire becomes fiery, and
> while remaining iron seems changed into fire . . . Union
> with God cannot exist otherwise than by participation with
> the Holy Spirit, diffusing in us the sanctification proper to
> Himself, imprinting and engraving on our souls the divine
> likeness.[6]

Didymus the blind man of Alexandria also insists strongly that God alone is able to communicate Himself to us substantially. He argues that such things as arts and sciences, virtues and vices dwell in us as accidental qualities and not as substances. But the indwelling of the Holy Spirit is His substantial Self as present and sanctifying.

> Now it is the proper substance of the Holy Spirit who dwells in the just and who sanctifies them and it belongs only to the Three Persons of the Holy Trinity, to be able, by their substance, to penetrate into souls.[7]

PRAYING IN THE SPIRIT

The Good News that Jesus came to give us is that the Kingdom of God is truly within us. It is the inner, hidden, dwelling presence of the Holy Spirit, given to us in Baptism in an embryonic relationship whereby through the inner operations of the Spirit upon us in faith, hope and love we become more and more aware that we live a new life in Christ Jesus.

This indwelling Holy Spirit teaches us how to pray deeply in the heart. He leads us beyond our idols constructed about God to live in the mystery of the circular movement of the Father, Son and Spirit inter-love relationships. He bears witness to our spirit that we are truly children of God. He teaches us a new language of praise and worship, so that prayer is no longer a thing we do before we do something else, but it is a constant attitude of being "toward" God who is now realized to be the ground of our being. The Spirit leads us into deeper contemplation and more intimate union with the Father through Jesus

Christ by purifying the heart through a constant spirit of
repentance. He destroys the spirit of the Pharaisee in the
synagogue and replaces it with that of the repentant
Publican who in reverence and sorrow cannot even lift his
face to God but strikes his breast and whispers: "God, be
merciful to me, a sinner" (Lk 18:14).

The Spirit leads us ever deeper into our heart where an
abiding sense of sorrow for sins and fear of ever losing the
loving mercy of God create a contrite, humble heart.
Broken in the spirit of egoism and independence, we
humbly turn in our poverty toward God. Stripped of our
own power to heal ourselves, we cry out for healing and
the Spirit of love brings it about on the deepest levels of
our being, in our "heart."

Because the Spirit is truly communicating within us
His personality as the bond of love between the Father and
Son, He teaches us to pray in spirit and truth by convincing
us through an outpouring of faith, hope and love that we
are truly God's children, divinized by grace, made participators of the divine nature (2 P 1:4). The sanctifying
Spirit makes us become what Jesus Christ is by nature. He
truly divinizes us, regenerating us with God's very own life.

In prayer the Holy Spirit continually reveals to us the
deeper meanings of the Word of God as revealed in Holy
Scripture. It becomes "something alive and active; it cuts
like any double-edged sworn but more finely:it can slip
through the place where the soul is divided from the spirit,
or joints from the marrow;it can judge the secret emotions
and thoughts. No created thing can hide from him;
everything is uncovered and open to the eyes of the one to
whom we must give account of ourselves" (Heb 4:12-13).

In such infusion of knowledge and understanding of

the Word of God, the Holy Spirit opens to us the treasures
of the mysteries of faith. God is alive and in process always
of revealing Himself through His Son in His Spirit. The
Spirit reveals to us all we need to know about the Father
and His Son, Jesus Christ. We begin to experience how
Christ lives in our hearts through faith and by being built
up on love, we "will with all the saints have strength to
grasp the breadth and the length, the height and the
depth" (Ep 3:18). We will be filled with the utter fullness
of God. And that fullness is experienced as flowing within
us and, in that oneness with the indwelling divine life, we
can easily discover this same "unconcealing" divine life all
about us in the surrounding world of men and things.

Such Christians cry out constantly for greater release
of the Holy Spirit in order that they may pray as they
should in the Holy Trinity. We are daily assured that if we
pray for this, the Heavenly Father will pour out abundantly His Spirit of love upon us (Lk 11:13). Through the outpouring of the Holy Spirit into our hearts, we are seized by
Him and given to Jesus Christ who, as the Way, the Truth
and the Life, leads us to the Father, all together dwelling
within us. The riches of the mysteries of God are inexhaustible like an abyss. Yet prayer becomes more an action
of yielding to the indwelling Spirit so as to enter into the
very movement of triadic life that is present and
dynamically exercising its life from within. It is to go
beyond images, words and even feelings to reach through
the indwelling Spirit a state of complete abandonment to
the Heavenly Father.

Totally surrendered to God we live only for Him as
each moment brings us an occasion to be a living gift back
to God as He gives himself to us in His triadic movement
of love. A new threshold of union with God has been

reached in such prayer of the heart under the guidance of the indwelling Holy Spirit, for we have passed through the dread of the purification of the senses. God has taken away from us all attachment to sense pleasures as we have learned to let go in the darkness of our inner poverty to be guided by the "luminous-dark" presence of the indwelling Trinity. Now nothing or no one can be the source of any attraction without a conscious submission of that relationship to God's holy will. God is finally, through the presence of the indwelling Spirit, becoming our God!

THE WORK OF THE INDWELLING SPIRIT

As the Spirit is the loving presence between the Father and the Son, He can be present to us only by His works of love. In the Old Testament He is the creative force of God moving into chaos, darkness and death. He draws the "void" into a sharing of God's being (Gn 1:2). He was a transforming power that in the anointing of kings fashioned them into servants to rule God's People. He was the "seeing voice" of the Prophets of old who foretold the messianic age.

Men were given new hearts by God's Spirit (Ez 36:26). God had prophesied that this living presence of His Spirit among His people would be poured out in a future age in great abundance (Jl 3:1-2). And within us through the growth of faith, hope and love in prayer we experience the first great work that the Spirit effects in our lives as He sanctifies and justifies us. St. Paul describes this transforming power of the Spirit in our hearts:

These are the sort of people some of you were once, but

now you have been washed clean, and sanctified and justified through the name of the Lord Jesus Christ and through the Spirit of our God (1 Co 6:11).

God, through the Spirit of love, removes our iniquities from us as far as the east is from the west (Ps 103:12). "I it is, I it is, who must blot out everything and not remember your sins" (Is 43:25). The Spirit witnesses in the depths of our hearts that in Christ's death, God condemned sin in the flesh (Rm 8:3). Jesus Christ has passed over from sin and death into a new creation. His new and glorious life living within us makes Him the New Adam and Lord of the Universe. He is capable in this exalted existence in glory of bestowing upon us this new life that He has received from the Spirit of His Father by revealing to us that we are forgiven our sins and have been established as children of His Father. The indwelling Spirit is God's life-giving "Breath" that the Risen Jesus is always breathing upon us.

Amidst so much darkness that still lives within us and outside of us, the Spirit reveals to us that God has saved us, "by means of the cleansing water of rebirth and by renewing us with the Holy Spirit which He has so generously poured over us through Jesus Christ our savior" (Tt 3:4-7). This indwelling Spirit of the Risen Christ brings us into direct contact with the spiritualized Body-Person of Jesus Risen who dwells also within us along with the Heavenly Father who Jesus promised would come with Him to abide in us as in a mansion (Jn 14:23).

FREEING PROCESS

We are always through the indwelling Spirit caught up in an on-going process of becoming God's children through the regeneration that the Spirit brings us, allowing us to be "born of the Spirit" (Jn 3:6). The light of the Spirit leads us out of all darkness and illusion. We are gradually enlightened by the light of His indwelling presence to know the truth that we are in Christ, a part of His Risen Body. That same Spirit that drove Jesus Christ to "pass over" from His own independence into total surrendering love to the Father on our behalf on the cross, reveals to us that Jesus, the image of the Father's love for us individually, still loves us with that infinity of love. "For me He died," cried St. Paul in a transforming knowledge given him by the Spirit that dwelt within him (Ga 2:20).

As we yield to such a dynamic love pouring over our consciousness and the deep layers of our unconscious, we experience a new freedom of being children of God, loved so immensely by God Himself. Fears and anxieties are shed as we experience new powers to love, to be "toward" God and ourselves and our neighbors. The dried bones from the chaotic past take on new life as the Spirit breathes gently over them. We come out of the past as an old man waking from the dream suddenly to find himself a youth, full of life and exciting hope of what will be.

An expanded consciousness floods my whole being as I feel the body, soul, spirit relationships within me come together in an integrated, whole person. "God, it is good to be alive and healthy!" I realize the Divine uncreated

Energies of God's triadic life flowing through me, in every part, on every level. I am a branch and God is the vine. I breathe in His breath. I am alive with His life. Like a butterfly, with wet, tightly-packed wings, I stretch upward towards the Heavenly Kingdom. The wings dry, strengthen, lift me aloft to new, dizzying heights of union with God.[8]

Freed from sin by the light of the indwelling Spirit of Jesus Risen, we no longer can wish to live in darkness. "No one who has been begotten by God sins; because God's seed remains inside him, he cannot sin when he has been begotten by God" (1 Jn 3:9). As the Spirit constantly reveals to us from within our true identity as children, loved infinitely by a perfect Father through Jesus Christ who has died for us, we can live each moment in Him and with Him. We can learn to accept our true identity that is a becoming unto the full, matured children of God as Jesus was. But this takes place only in the present *now* that is the only *locus*, the meeting-place of God's eternal *now* of His love for us in Christ Jesus. The Holy Spirit progressively brings about our regeneration as children of God to the degree that we yield to His illuminations and inspiration, poured forth from within us. These give us knowledge and the power of love to live according to the revealed knowledge that the Spirit pushes us at each moment to live, namely, that we possess an inner dignity as children of God, one with Christ, a part of His very Body.

St. Augustine, commenting on the words of Ps. 82: "You too are gods, sons of the Most High, all of you" (v.6), expresses well our human dignity as children of God:

He who justifies is the very same who deifies, because in justifying us He makes us children of God . . . Now, if we are children of God, by that very fact we are gods, doubtless not by a natural generation, but a grace of adoption. One holy, indeed, is the Son of God by nature, the one only God with the Father, our Lord and Savior Jesus Christ . . . The others who become gods so become by His grace; they are not born of His substance so as to become what He is, but they attain to a divine sonship by the favor of His generosity, in order that they may be made co-heirs of Christ.[9]

We are, according to St. Paul, alive by the Spirit, so we must walk always by the Spirit. "If you are guided by the Spirit you will be in no danger of yielding to self-indulgence . . . the Spirit is totally against such a thing . . . If you are led by the Spirit, no law can touch you" (Ga 5:16-18).

FRUIT OF THE SPIRIT

The presence of the Holy Spirit within us is not a delectation to be enjoyed without any reference to daily living and growth into greater life as children of God. The indwelling Spirit prods us to greater complexity, to greater pruning and inner discipline. For with St. Paul, we all continually realize that we are caught within the dialectic of two forces: the power of darkness and evil and that of the Spirit of Jesus which is holiness and light. We are to live according to the Spirit of Jesus. This Spirit creates the new life of Christ within us. He also fosters and brings it to its fullness in the proportion that the Spirit becomes normative in guiding the Christians to make choices according to the mind of Christ. Ideally the life of a Christian is freed from any extrinsic legalism and is guided by that interior communication that he receives when he turns within and listens to the Spirit of Jesus.

By the spirit produced we Christians have no doubt as to which spirit is guiding us — the spirit of the world or the Spirit of the Risen Jesus. St. Paul described these two opposite sets of fruit. He ends up describing the authentic fruit of the Holy Spirit:

> What the Spirit brings is very different:love, joy, peace, patience, kindness, goodness, trustfullness, gentleness and self-control. There can be no law against these things like that, of course. You cannot belong to Christ Jesus unless you crucify all self-indulgent passions and desires. Since the Spirit is our life, let us be directed by the Spirit (Ga 5:22-25).

It is through the Spirit that God who is love is able to communicate to us the power to be loving, filled with joy, abounding in patience and in general, putting on the mind of Christ in all thoughts, words and deeds. The work of the Spirit that dwells within us is to pour out the love of God into our hearts since He is given to us (Rm 5:5). The outpouring of the Spirit is the filling up in our hearts of the love of God. What is impossible to us who still carry sin in our members (Rm 7:23) becomes possible by the indwelling Spirit. We are able to love at each moment with the very love of God that abides within us. "Anyone who lives in love lives in God, and God lives in him" (1 Jn 4:16). The love of God through the Spirit gradually possesses our heart. It is the same love with which God the Father loves His Son and ourselves as His children. We are to yield to

this inner power and live in it in all our human relationships. The Holy Spirit dwelling within us is the love of God
abiding in us and empowering us to become loving human
beings. It is in the power of the Holy Spirit that we can be
loving.

To attain this union of active love with Jesus Christ,
the Spirit of Jesus reveals to us how we are to do always all
actions to please God, to lead "a life acceptable to Him in
all its aspects" (Col 1:10). But this cannot be done unless
we are ready to put to death our carnal desires and put on
the mind of Christ. It is the Spirit that helps us. "The
Spirit too comes to help us in our weakness" (Rm 8:26).
The Spirit prays by allowing us to be present to the
Father's overwhelming love for us. But above all, the
Spirit pours out this divine love into our hearts. It is by the
Spirit's love infused into us that we can die to selfishness
and live to Christ. Through the love of God poured into
our hearts we can be always patient and kind, never jealous
or boastful or conceited or rude or selfish. We need no
more to take offense or be resentful. We will always be
ready to excuse, to trust, to hope and to endure whatever
comes. For love is the greatest gift of God. It is truly the
Holy Spirit Himself operating freely within us (1 Co
13:4-13).

SENT TO BUILD COMMUNITY

The Holy Spirit brings us into a deep union with Jesus
Christ so that His name is always on our lips and in our
hearts. Our life becomes a *oneness* in Him as we seek to
live each moment in the transcendence of the Risen Jesus.
This is the work of the Spirit:

And we, with our unveiled faces reflecting like mirrors the brightness of the Lord, all grow brighter and brighter as we are turned into the image that we reflect; this is the work of the Lord who is Spirit (2 Co 3:18).

Through the experience that is always on-going of being one in Christ, living members of His very Body, the Spirit prompts us outward, not only to discover Christ in others, but to labor incessantly to bring Jesus forth in their lives. The Spirit is the builder of the Body of Christ. "There is one Body, one Spirit, just as you were all called into one and the same hope when you are called" (Ep 4:4).

We see that in the life of Jesus, whenever the Spirit is associated with Him, it is in the light of His mission. His mission was to fight against the world and its sinfulness and to conquer it. When Jesus preached in the synagogue in Nazareth, He read from Is 61:1-2.

He has sent me to bring the good news to the poor,
to proclaim liberty to captives
and to the blind new sight,
to set the downtrodden free,
to proclaim the Lord's year of favor (Lk 4:18).

This was the mission and He was anointed in His baptism by St. John the Baptist for this work of setting us free. The Spirit anointed Him to preach, to heal and perform miracles. And He pours out His Spirit upon His followers that they might also be anointed by the Spirit for a sharing in the mission of Jesus.

'As the Father sent me,
so am I sending you.'

After saying this he breathed on them and said:
'Receive the Holy Spirit.
For those whose sins you forgive,
they are forgiven;
for those whose sins you retain,
they are retained' (Jn 20:21-23).

The Spirit is poured into our hearts not only that we
might rejoice in the good news that we are God's children
but that we might go out and bring the good news that all
human beings are called by God to become through the
Spirit of love also God's children. Jesus is to extend His
anointed work through His Spirit poured out into His
members in order to take away sins, liberate mankind from
all effects of sins and to bring about a new creation that
will be the reconciliation of the entire world to the Father
in fulfillment of His eternal plan in creating all things in
and through His word. "It was God who reconciled us to
himself through Christ and gave us the work of handing on
this reconciliation . . . So we are ambassadors for Christ; it
is as though God were appealing through us, and the appeal that we make in Christ's name is: be reconciled to
God" (2 Co 5:18-20).

St. Paul writes to the Corinthian Church that the
various members have been given diverse gifts by the
Spirit, all to build up the Body of Christ.

There is a variety of gifts but always the same Spirit; there
are all sorts of service to be done, but always to the same
Lord; working in all sorts of different ways in different
people, it is the same God who is working in all of them.
The particular way in which the Spirit is given to each person is for a good purpose . . . All these are the work of one

and the same Spirit, who distributes different gifts to different people just as he chooses (1 Co 12:4-11).

St. Paul gives here a list of nine gifts or charisms that serve to build up an individual, praying community. In Rm 12:6-8 he gives another, broader list of charisms, but all are to build up the one Body, the Church, whose Head is Christ and whose members are Christians in whom dwells the Holy Spirit. The Spirit gives all of us charisms for the good of the whole Body, the Church. In Ep 4:11-13, St. Paul gives still another list along the lines of hierarchical functions.

But what the indwelling Spirit within us reveals is that our proper dignity as children of God consists in our functioning within the Body of Christ out of love to serve the whole community. The sign of true Christian maturity into the "new man" (Ep 2:5; 4:24) is our readiness to put aside our egoism and live for the good of the whole. It is according to the degree of conscious, corporate unity with Christ, the Head, and all of the members that each individual grows in perfection and can assist in building up the whole Body. "If we live by the truth and in love, we shall grow in all ways into Christ, who is the Head" (Ep 4:15).

The fruit that we are called to bring forth within the Body of Christ is love for each other, which again, as we have seen, is the principal fruit of the indwelling Spirit. We know that Jesus Christ lives in each of us as is shown in the love that we show towards all men; this is possible only through the work of the Spirit within us. It is this truth that we have comprehended by the help of the Spirit of the indwelling Jesus who sets us free (Jn 8:32).

POWER OF THE HOLY SPIRIT

Jesus had promised that He would ask the Father to send the Spirit of truth upon His followers (Jn 14:15-29) to be with them, in the Church, in each Christian, and to stay with them forever. This Spirit is meant not merely to abide within us believers, but to send us forth in love as He is being sent forth in love by the Father and the Son. The Spirit would teach the followers of Jesus everything and would bring to their consciousness everything that Jesus had said and done (Jn 14:25-27).

The Spirit would teach Christians about Jesus and would empower them to become witnesses of Jesus, just as the Spirit witnesses to Him (Jn 15:26). This same Spirit will unfold, reveal the plan of salvation to the believers in Jesus and give them true judgment according to Christ's plan. The world's sin is disbelief. The Spirit will expose that and will lead the followers of Jesus into the complete truth (Jn 16:7-15).

Jesus had to leave His Disciples in order to be freed from space and time to exist in a new form. After His resurrection He would be able to abide within His followers along with His Father and His Spirit (Jn 14:23). He would give them a new baptism with the Holy Spirit (Ac 1:5), and the great promise that Jesus continues to make to all of us modern Christians as He made it to His Apostles: " . . . you will receive power when the Holy Spirit comes on you, and then you will be my witnesses not only in Jerusalem but throughout Judaea and Samaria, and indeed to the ends of the earth" (Ac 1:8).

After Pentecost when they had received the outpouring of the Holy Spirit, the first Christian community in

Jerusalem witnessed to what, like the Apostles, we also could receive: filled with the Spirit, they went forth to witness to the inner transformation that took place through their baptism by Jesus in the Holy Spirit. They preached and witnessed fearlessly to the Risen Jesus. They performed signs and miracles. St. Peter confesses to the astonished Jews: ". . . what you see and hear is the outpouring of that Spirit" (Ac 2:33).

As we read the *Acts of the Apostles* and the epistles of St. Paul, we see the power of the Spirit that came upon the followers of Jesus. They pray for courage and power to preach the message, to heal and work miracles through the name of Jesus and they received that power (Ac 4:29-31). The early community remained faithful to the teaching of the Apostles, to the brotherhood, to the breaking of bread and to prayers. They shared everything in common and worked miracles and signs and God blessed their community with new members (Ac 2:42-47).

If problems arose, they consulted the Spirit within them and within the *koinonia* or Christian brotherhood. "It has been decided by the Holy Spirit and by ourselves . . ." (Ac 15:28). They seek the mind of God through the Spirit's guidance in prayer and fasting (Ac 13:2). "We and the Holy Spirit" (Ac 5:32) becomes the continued experience within that early Church, the fruit of Jesus sending upon those who believe in Him the Holy Spirit. Stephen and Philip, deacons, are filled with the Spirit and preach and work miracles with great power. Converts from among not only Jews but also the Gentiles are brought into the Church by the Holy Spirit being given to them when they are prayed over by the elders.

CONFRONTING THE WORLD WITH THE SPIRIT

Jesus sends us the Spirit in order that sin, the result of the world's darkness in us, be eradicated from us. But the Spirit within us drives us out into the world to confront the chaos, darkness and death that exist there. The life in the Spirit is to be a life of struggle and fight against sin in whatever form it appears, in our own personal lives or in those of others or in the society in which we live. The world cannot accept the Spirit since it neither sees nor recognizes Him (Jn 14:17). There is an aggressive hostility on the part of the world against the Spirit and the work of Christ to restore unity in the human race. The world will hate the disciples of Christ and persecute them (Jn 15:18-20).

But the Christians in the Spirit are not to run away from the world but are to be the "ambassadors of Christ," bearing the Word of God. The Spirit dwells within us (Jn 14:17) and we are to be Christ's witnesses to His values of the Gospel by our lives lived in brotherly love and unity. We are to be led by the Spirit of love. To refuse to be led by this Spirit is sin. Even when persons unknowingly operate out of transcendent, self-forgetting love, they are being guided by the Spirit. To sin is to assert self over the Spirit of love that lives for loving service toward the others.

The Spirit of love, God's love, has been operating in the Old Testament times, but also among all men of good will outside of the Old and New Covenants. God has poured His Spirit of love into the hearts of all men who willingly submit to live for the Absolute God in loving service to their neighbors. This Spirit of love operates in the most simple things of life: in the act of giving a cup of cold water to a traveler, a letter written to a loved one,

visiting the lonely and sickly. His unifying force is felt in all
technological and medical advances brought about by
human beings cooperating with the uncreated energies of
God's love, found in every facet of human living.

This Spirit of the Risen Christ is operating in the lives
of a man and woman deeply in love who experience this
divine, unifying force of love in their conjugal union as
they leave selfish *eros* to find their own beings and to ex-
pand by giving without reserve to the other to bring forth
in that outflowing energy of life a new life, made to the image and likeness of God Himself. This is creativity at its
highest, union through *agape*, the truest sign of the presence of the Spirit.

This Spirit is working as a mother and father work patiently to form their child, as a religious or lay persons
teach students, as professional workers, skilled and un-
skilled men and women, do their daily work with loving
dedication to fellow man. Such persons in their work experience a true dedication to fellow man. Such persons in
their very work experience a true liberation, an expansion
of their inner being, a resurrection to a new and higher
level of life in the Spirit of Jesus Christ. This may be consciously in the performance of our "secular" actions. Yet
the law of the Spirit holds true in all cases: to "ascend" to
a higher form of existence, a greater liberation, a new level
of oneness in love with others with a new consciousness of
our own individuated personhood, we must undergo a
"descending" process. This is a dying to the elements in
our total make-up that act as obstacles to the operations of
the indwelling Spirit.

In all details of our lives the Spirit of God is operating

to effect the one desire of God in our regard: "What God wants is for you all to be holy" (1 Th 4:3). For this purpose God . . .·"gives you his Holy Spirit" (1 Th 4:8). There is no area of our lives that is not touched at every moment by the Spirit of the Risen Jesus. No area of our lives lies in the strictly "profane," which means, that all things belong to God's Spirit of love. The Spirit of God fills the whole world. He holds all things together (Heb 1:3; Col 1:17). He is present to all human beings, communicating God's great love for them and drawing them into a greater image-likeness to His Son, Jesus Christ.

> The spirit of the Lord, indeed, fills the whole world, and that which holds all, things together knows every word that is said. The man who gives voice to injustice will never go unnoticed, nor shall avenging Justice pass him by (Wi 1:7-8).

Peter De Rosa well describes the working of the Spirit among those who serve others in love, whether they do it knowingly or unknowingly in the Spirit of love:

> Whoever rights wrongs, feeds the hungry, cares for the dispossessed not merely with enthusiasm but with dogged determination, whoever is meek and poor of heart; whoever is sensitive towards the numerous little heartaches people suffer, is—knowingly or unknowingly—an envoy of Christ. And whoever shares in Christ's mission, shares in the Fire of the Spirit.[10]

BE FILLED WITH THE SPIRIT

St. Paul gives this as a command to those who are followers of Christ by choice and God's grace. "Be filled with the Spirit" (Ep 5:18). This is the end of our lives. Each moment of each day we must desire to be baptized by Jesus Christ in His Holy Spirit.

Each time we choose to surrender ourselves to the inner guidance, the Spirit assuredly gives us an infusion of faith, hope and love. When such surrendering becomes habitual we can call it infused contemplation, the gift of the Holy Spirit whereby He gives to our spiritual faculties of understanding and willing, of knowing and loving, an habitual experience of the transcendent God, Father, Son and Spirit, immanently present within us and drawing us into a union of His triadic family. In this prayerful, adoring communion an intense union of wills takes place. We feel *one* with the Trinity. The Three Persons, Father, Son and Spirit, are constantly present to us and we to them in loving surrender.

Yet along with the heightened sense of oneness with God, the Spirit gives us a new understanding of our *uniqueness*. We know our identity in God's Spirit of love. In saying *I* to the *Thou* of God, we know in a new awareness how individually and beautifully we are loved by God. "I have called thee by thy name. Thou art mine" (Is 43:1). We experience the loving gaze of the Heavenly Father, imaged by the presence of Jesus Christ, His only begotten Son who is always giving Himself unto the last drop of blood on the cross. In their look of love we spring into *new* being. The Trinity's personalized love, experienced now more deeply and more totally (less conceptually), calls us to be the unique person God wishes us to be.

Such a person can afford to give his life away and truly finds it in his gift of love to another. We step out into life's fast-moving stream and eagerly embrace each moment as a *now* moment of growing in greater love for God and neighbor. Each person, thing, event encountered becomes an epiphany, a manifestation of God appearing in our lives in a new incarnational form. As the Spirit was present, hovering over Mary in the Incarnation, so the same Spirit hovers over each moment to "unconceal" for us through faith, hope and love the loving, incarnational presence of Jesus Christ who leads us to the Father.

Nothing surprises us or upsets us, because the Spirit's quickening of faith, hope and love allows us to see "inside" of all things and there to discover God's loving action. We see that all things really work unto good to those who love the Lord (Rm 8:28). Praise comes to our lips readily as we see God in a diaphany, a shining through, each happening of each moment.

To live in such a mystical union with the Trinity is impossible by our own powers. But it is the Spirit that teaches us how to pray as we ought (Rm 8:26-27). It should not be considered an extraordinary state of prayer for anyone who sincerely wishes to be continually baptized by Jesus Christ in His Spirit. We can all receive the gift of contemplation that is a process of continued growth in loving submission to Jesus Christ as Lord. But this is impossible without the Spirit (1 Co 12:3). God wishes us all to grow in mystical union with the Trinity.

We are all called by Jesus Christ in His Spirit to enter into a consciousness of communing with the Holy Trinity that knows no interruption. For such who grow in the baptism in the Holy Spirit, this admits of a continued increase in awareness of the immanence of the indwelling Trinity within them. As they yield themselves in each moment to the uncreated energies of God divinizing them into children of God, they become more vitally aware through the indwelling Spirit that they are loved as children by an infinitely loving Father.

The true test of what degree of contemplation we have reached is tested by the life we live. If we are aware of the indwelling Spirit who leads us to a living knowledge and love of the Father and Jesus Christ, then we are truly made by that Spirit's power into new creatures in Christ Jesus (2 Co 5:17). This new state of being in Christ will show itself consistently in our lives through the love we have toward one another and by the humility we manifest in authentic service to meet their needs. True mysticism of the indwelling Trinity and true baptism in the Holy Spirit will always be measured by the degree that we allow the Spirit to transfigure us into love which must then go out into a loving service toward others. True love of God will always be a true love for other human beings. Ultimately there can be only one love and that is the Spirit of the Trinity bringing forth within us the relationship that we can call "graced-love." The truly charismatic Christian, baptized in the Spirit continuously in the circumstances of his daily life, is a mystic who has been transformed into a living incarnation of God's love for mankind.

Let us love one another since love comes from God
And everyone who loves is begotten by God and knows
God.

Anyone who fails to love can never have known God.
As long as we love one another God will live in us
And His love will be complete in us . . .
God is love and anyone who lives in love
    lives in God
And God lives in him (1 Jn 4:7-16).

I SURRENDER

I pray alone
on the mountain tops of night.
It is so calm, so still.
All is dark;
yet coming closer and closer
to me is a robe
of great brilliance.
I close my eyes in fear.
As the full-sun,
He stops before me,
dazzling, dancing.
His presence pierces
through my whole being
yet consuming me not.
I kiss the earth before Brilliance.
I let go and fly to ecstasy.
Oh, God, before such beauty
I surrender!

Rev. George A. Maloney, S.J.

8

Communion With The Holy Trinity

After the mass suicides at Jonestown in Guyana, psychologists were busy analyzing what causes people to surrender, not only their money and their privacy, but even the control over their lives to such a point that a leader like Jim Jones could demand hundreds of his followers to join him in committing suicide. Many of these psychologists have suggested that deep-rooted needs, stemming from an insecure childhood, made it easy for a cult leader, such as Jones, to control his followers as though they were puppets with no freedom to do anything but his will.

One psychologist, Dr. Arthur Janov, extends the "cult" phenomenon to include all religions. In a rather biased and unscientific generalization he writes:

> Are the cultists crazy? Yes, but no more so than any other true believers or converts. Religion is one form of socially institutionalized insanity. It is the best kind because the follower is never alone in it. His unreality is affirmed constantly by everyone around him. Followers can get together in the fields and chant, say litanies, sing together and believe in the savior—the one who saved them from reality.[1]

Human saviors often can forget that they are not also divine but merely human beings. When such a human savior is carried away by his own need for power, there is the possibility of a cult that will de-humanize lives. But Christians precisely call Jesus Christ their Savior because He was both divine and human. He was not sinful and, therefore, did not need to use people for His own power. He emptied Himself of all power and was meek and humble of heart. And the sign of His disciples was that they also would be gentle and kind, loving one another as He loves us.

Christians believe that Jesus Christ, God-become-man, came among us in order to free us from unreality or the darkness of self-centeredness by pouring out the Spirit of His Father's love into our hearts. By the power of such experienced, divine love, Christians are brought into a new creation. The old "reality" disappears and the Christian who lives in Christ Jesus now knows true reality. St. Paul put it thus:

> From now onwards, therefore, we do not judge anyone by the standards of the flesh . . . And for anyone who is in Christ, there is a new creation; the old creation has gone, and now the new one is here (2 Co 5:16-17).

Jesus Himself claimed that He came to bring us life and that more abundantly (Jn 10:10). And He described that life as eternal and as a knowing experience of the Father and the Son (Jn 17:3). Such knowledge was to be experienced as an ongoing process of God's infinite love for us human beings by giving us His only begotten Son (Jn 3:16).

RECAPITULATION THROUGH JESUS CHRIST

We have seen in previous chapters how God's essence as love seeks always to share itself with others. His divine plan was that He would communicate His Word by assuming flesh. Into Jesus Christ, fully God and fully man, the Trinity, Source of all reality, pours itself. God channels all of His life through Him "because God wanted all perfection to be found in him and all things to be reconciled through him and for him" (Col 1:19). St. Paul tells us: "In his body lives the fullness of divinity and in him you too find your own fulfillment" (Col 2:9).

Jesus is the reconciler of all things in the heavens and on the earth. He will restore the world's lost unity as He draws men and women by the loving attraction of His Spirit into His very Body. He at the time of His death and resurrection, in microcosm as it were, re-established or reconciled humanity in Himself by destroying sin, death and the distorted element in the flesh. The Trinity exalted Him in glory (Ph 2:9-11), making Him the "first born among many brethren" (Rm 8:29). At the end of time He will also re-establish all things, raising up the flesh of all mankind by spiritualizing it. He will bring all things completely under His dominion by bestowing the fullness of His divine life upon men for all eternity.

But this re-establishing of divine life in the individual human being is a process that has already begun through Baptism and the increase of the Spirit's gifts of faith, hope and love. As we human beings surrender our lives to Jesus Christ, we find in Him the center of unity, harmony and meaningfulness which gives to us and the entire world its sense and its value. This is true reality. Jesus becomes the meeting point of God and His creation. The infinite, burning love of God's goodness meets in Him and ignites that love in our hearts. We are to ignite love, then, in the hearts of all we meet.

This meeting of the triune life in Christ begins in Baptism. "All baptised in Christ, you have all clothed yourselves in Christ" (Ga 3:27). We share in His fullness (Jn 1:16). This divine life grows unto ever increasing perfection through the other sacraments, especially Confirmation. "In the one Spirit we were all baptised, . . . and one Spirit was given to us all to drink" (1 Co 12:13).

THE GIFT OF THE EUCHARIST

Our centering in Christ and our entrance into the fullness of the trinitarian life reach their peak of perfection in the Eucharist. In the Eucharist we open ourselves to the ultimate presence of the uncreated energies of God along with the personalized acts of the three Persons. It is Christ's resurrected body that comes to man in Holy Communion. But through this "Way," we are led into the holy presence of the Trinity. Now Jesus Christ, the eternal Word of God, the Second Person of the Trinity, can never be separated from His divinized humanity. It is the whole Jesus Christ that comes to us and this glorified God-Man can never be separated from the Father and the Holy Spirit relationships.

St. Gregory of Nyssa compares Jesus in the Eucharist to a leaven that "assimilates to itself the whole lump, so in like manner that body to which immortality has been given by God, when it is in ours, translates and transmutes the whole into itself."[2] He argues that Christ, through His Eucharistic Body, can vivify the whole of mankind just as the same divine power changed the physical bread that Jesus Christ ate into the Body of God. Instead of the consumed food becoming part of the person eating it, the eater is transformed into the divine nourishment.[3]

In the Incarnation God so loved the world as to give us His only begotten Son (Jn 3:16); out of this mystery of His infinite love for us flows the Eucharist. As the gift of the Eucharist is possible only because of the gift of the God-Man, the Logos-made-flesh in the Incarnation, so the mystery of the Incarnation leads us ultimately to the mystery of the Blessed Trinity. Who sees the Son sees also the Father (Jn 14:9). Who receives the body and blood of the Son of God receives not only the Son but also the Father in His Spirit of love. Who abides in the Son abides in the Father who comes with the Son and His Spirit to dwell within the recipient of the Eucharist (Jn 14:23).

Thus all three mysteries of the Eucharist, the Incarnation and the Trinity are intimately connected and explain each other. The mysteries of the Trinity and the Incarnation are rooted in God's essence as Love. As the Trinity seeks to share its very own intimate, "family" life with others, the Word leaps forth from out of the heart of the Father. "For when peaceful stillness compassed everything and the night in its swift course was half spent, your all-powerful word from heaven's royal throne bounded, a fierce warrior into the doomed land" (Wi 18:14-15).

God's Word inserts Himself into our material world, taking upon Himself the form of a servant (Ph 2:8), like to us in all things save sin (Heb 4:15). Not only does God wed Himself to the entire, material universe by assuming matter into the trinitarian family, but God also touches each human being. Through the Incarnation all human beings are made one through the humanity of Jesus Christ. He is the *New Adam*, the true Father of the human race. We are destined to live with Him and through Him the very life that was that of God's only begotten Son.

The Eucharist brings this oneness with Christ to fulfillment. Our relationship to the Trinity is not one of an extrinsic adoption, analogous to the true, natural sonship of Jesus Christ. In giving us in the Eucharist His very body and blood as food and drink, Jesus Christ wishes to share His very own life with us.

As I, who am sent by the living Father,
myself draw life from the Father,
so whoever eats me will draw life from me.
This is the bread come down from heaven;
not like the bread our ancestors ate:
they are dead,
but anyone who eats this bread will live for ever (Jn 6:57-58).

The Father has the fullness of life and He has communicated it to His Son. Jesus Christ, the Image of the Father in human form, pours His very own life into all of us who wish to partake of His flesh and blood. He is the "Living Bread," the Bread of Life that comes down from Heaven. In the Incarnation He took upon Himself our human flesh. In the Eucharist we become assimilated into

His human-divine nature.

It is staggering to our weak human minds and impossible to comprehend adequately the depths of God the Father's love for us as imaged in His only begotten Son. It is *in fact* that we become one with God's only Son. We are *engrafted* into His very being as a branch is inserted into the mainstream of the vine and becomes one total being (Jn 15:1-6).

St. John Chrysostom perceives this amazing mystery and accentuates the fact of our oneness in the Eucharist with Jesus Christ.

> . . . . Therefore in order that we may become of His Body, not in desire only, but also in very fact, let us become commingled with that Body. This, in truth, takes place by means of the food which He has given us as a gift, because He desired to prove the love which He has for us. It is for this reason that He has shared Himself with us and has brought His Body down to our level, namely, that we might be one with Him as the body is joined with the head.
>
> And to show the love He has for us He has made it possible for those who desire, not merely to look upon Him, but even to touch Him and to consume Him and to fix their teeth in His Flesh and to be commingled with Him; in short, to fulfill all their love. Let us then, come back from that table like lions breathing out fire, thus becoming terrifying to the Devil and remaining mindful of our Head and of the love which He has shown us.[4]

INCORPORATION INTO CHRIST

The Greek Fathers had grasped this union with Christ in the Eucharist to be a literal union, a true incorporation into Christ's very own substance. This doctrine they saw as nothing but a commentary on the Pauline and Johannine theology of union with Christ through Baptism and Eucharist. It was St. Paul who especially developed the doctrine of incorporation into Christ's own life. As the Apostle to the Gentiles, he boldly developed this key teaching that made Christianity essentially different from paganism. Through the cross Christ destroyed eschatological death and sin. By His own resurrectional life He brought to us this "new life." "When He died, he died, once for all, to sin, so his life now is life with God; and in that way, you too must consider yourselves to be dead to sin but alive for God in Christ Jesus" (Rm 6:10-11).

But for us to become "alive to God in Christ Jesus," we must be united with Christ; we must be *in Christ*. St. Paul uses this phrase *in Christ* 164 times and he usually means by this a very real, intimate union with Christ. Baptism puts us into direct contact with the resurrected, glorified Christ who now, by His spiritualized Body-Person, can come and truly dwell within us, especially through the Eucharist.

> The blessing-cup that we bless is a communion with the blood of Christ, and the bread that we break is a communion with the body of Christ. The fact that there is only one loaf means that, though there are many of us, we form a single body because we all have a share in this one loaf (1 Co 10:16-17).

We share in the Eucharist in Christ's own life, that life of the historical person, Jesus Christ, now gloriously resurrected. We are personally incorporated into Christ, without losing our own identity. Christ lives in us, but we must always be further formed in Him (Ga 4:19). By yielding to the life-giving influence of Christ, we Christians are gradually transformed into the image of Christ. This is the only plan and destiny of God, namely, that we are to be transformed into the image of the only-begotten Son, Jesus Christ. "They are the one he chose specially long ago and intended to become true images of his Son, so that his Son might be the eldest of many brothers. He called those he intended for this, those he called he justified, and with those he justified he shared his glory" (Rm 8:29-30).

In the Eucharist Jesus Christ comes to us with the fullness of His divine and human natures. He opens to us "the unsearchable riches of Christ" (Ep 3:8). He loves us in the oneness of the infinite, uncreated energies of love of the Trinity. We join our hearts to that of the God-Man and praise and worship the Heavenly Father with a perfect love and complete self-surrender.

UNION WITH THE TRINITY

In our oneness with Jesus Christ in the Eucharist we are brought into the heart of the Trinity. Here is the climax of God's eternal plan when he "chose us in Christ, to be holy and spotless, and to live through love in his presence" (Ep 1:4). Sin destroys that imageness and likeness to Jesus Christ within us. Our own sinfulness, added to the effects of original sin, hinders the Holy Spirit to raise us to an awareness in grace that Jesus truly lives in us and we in Him. But the Eucharist (and here we see the need of preparation to receive worthily this sacrament, for repentance and an authentic *metanoia* or conversion) restores and powerfully builds up this oneness with Christ.

Along with an intensification of our own I-Thou relationship with Jesus Christ, the Holy Spirit brings us into a new awareness of our being also one with the Father and His Holy Spirit. This is the essence of the Last Supper Discourse of Jesus as recorded in St. John's Gospel.

I pray not only for these,
but for those also
who through their words will believe in me.
May they all be one.
Father, may they be one in us,
as you are in me and I am in you,
so that the world may believe it was you who sent me.
I have given them the glory you gave to me,
that they may be one as we are one.
With me in them and you in me,
may they be so completely one
that the world will realize that it was you who sent me
and that I have loved them as much as you loved me
    (Jn 17:20-23).

The glory that the Father gave to Jesus was to raise through the Incarnation His human nature into a oneness with His "natural" state of being the only begotten Son of the Father from all eternity. That same glory in the Eucharist Jesus is sharing with us to be by the power of the Holy Spirit one with His Sonship. We are raised to a supernatural relationship to the Blessed Trinity. We become by the fruit of the Eucharist, as the Byzantine Liturgy of St. John Chrysostom puts it, "through the fellowship of the Holy Spirit," true participators of God's very own nature (2 P 1:4).

St. Cyril of Alexandria clearly grasped not only our

divinization as children of God through the Eucharist[6] but also our own union with the Trinity.

> Accordingly we are all one in the Father and in the Son and in the Holy Spirit; one, I say, in unity of relationship of love and concord with God and one another, . . . one by conformity in godliness, by communion in the sacred body of Christ, and by fellowship in the one and Holy Spirit and this is a real, physical union.[7]

For if we receive, as we truly believe, the total Jesus Christ, true God and true man, we also receive the Father and His Spirit. For the Son cannot be separated from the glorious union He enjoys with the Father. This is more than a moral union. The Son has received everything that He is from the Father. Unlike an earthly father who can sire a child and thereafter is no longer a substantial union, the Heavenly Father is thereafter continuously pouring the fullness of His being into His Son. Jesus clearly taught ". . . . that I am in the Father and the Father is in me" (Jn 14:10). More clearly yet, Jesus said: ". . . he who sent me is with me, and has not left me to myself" (Jn 8:29).

If Jesus and the Father abide in each other and have come to abide within us in the Eucharist (Jn 14:23), the Holy Spirit, as the bond of unity that brings them together and who proceeds as love from their abiding union, also comes and dwells in us. How fittingly are St. Paul's words applied to our reception of the Eucharist: "Your body, you know, is the temple of the Holy Spirit, who is in you since you received him from God" (1 Co 6:19). Again St. Paul describes the indwelling Spirit as accompanying the love of God in our hearts: " . . . the love of God has been poured into our hearts by the Holy Spirit which has been given us" (Rm 5:5).

Just as the Holy Spirit was present in the Incarnation effecting a begetting by the Father of His Son in human form (Lk 1;35), so the Holy Spirit is present in two ways in the Eucharist. The first way is highlighted in most of the Eastern Liturgies and is called the *epiklesis.* This literally means a "calling down" of the Holy Spirit to bless and transform the gifts of bread and wine into the body and blood of Jesus Christ. "Send down your Holy Spirit upon us and upon these gifts lying before us . . . and make this bread the precious Body of your Christ, Amen. And that which is in this chalice the precious Blood of your Christ, Amen. Having changed them by your Holy Spirit, Amen, Amen, Amen. (The Liturgies of St. Basil and St. John Chrysostom).

The second presence of the Holy Spirit is the bond of unity between the Father and the Son and all who receive Jesus Christ. This is called the *koinonia* or *fellowship* or communion of the Holy Spirit. This fruit of the Eucharist, prayed for in the Eastern Liturgies, is mentioned by St. Paul: "The grace of the Lord Jesus Christ, the love of God and the fellowship of the Holy Spirit be with you all" (2 Co 13:13).

CHILDREN OF GOD

The treasure that the Holy Spirit gives to us in the Eucharist is oneness with the family of God. "What we have seen and heard we are telling you so that you too may be in fellowship with us, as we are in union with the Father and with his Son Jesus Christ" (1 Jn 1:3). We are in union with the Trinity because the Holy Spirit is poured out to us through the glorified humanity of Jesus in the Eucharist. But that union is effected by the Holy Spirit who raises our human natures to a true sonship and daughtership with the Father by the oneness we enjoy in the Eucharist with the only begotten Son of God. We are truly children of God.

> Everyone moved by the Spirit is a son of God. The Spirit you received is not the spirit of slaves bringing fear into your lives again; it is the spirit of sons, and it makes us cry out, 'Abba, Father!' The Spirit himself and our spirit bear united witness that we are children of God, and if we are children we are heirs as well:heirs of God and co-heirs with Christ, sharing his sufferings so as to share his glory (Rm 8:14-17; also, Ga 4:6-7; Jn 14:15-17; 14:26; 15:27; 16:7-11; 16:13-14).

In the Eucharist *par excellence* we experience the Father begetting us in His one Son through His Spirit. "You are my son, today I have become your father" (Ps 2:7). In a way, we can say that the Father loves only one person and that is His own Son, Jesus Christ. But he loves us with an infinite love as He loves us in Him. What reverence ought to be ours as we open our hearts to the perfect love of Jesus for His Father! What joy should flood us as we experience an infinite love of the Father being generated freshly for us in each Eucharistic reception as He loves us in Jesus!

St. Hilary of Poitiers encourages the communicant, who is joined to the Father through Christ to press on to greater union with the Father. For "Christ Himself is in us by His flesh and we are in Him, while all that we are is with Him in God."[9]

We are more than merely adopted children of God. As

has been pointed out earlier through contact with the humanity of Christ, the Eucharist through the Holy Spirit effects a union between us and God that makes us truly sharers of God's very divine nature. St. Symeon the new Theologian (+1022) expresses this awesome mystery:

> . . . I receive in Communion
> the Body divinized as being that of God.
> I too become god
> in this inexpressible union.
> See what a mystery!
> The soul then and the body . . .
> are one being in two essences.
> Therefore these are one and two
> in communion with Christ
> and drinking His blood,
> they are united to two essences,
> united in this way to the essences of my God,
> they become god by participation.
> They are called by the same name as that of Him
> in whom they have participated on a level of essence.
> They say that coal is fire
> and the iron is black.
> Yet when the iron is immersed in the fire
> it appears as fire.
> If it then appears as such,
> we also can call it by that name.
> We see it as fire,
> we can call it fire.[10]

We are received into the only begotten Son of God by an *ontological* union, a unique oneness with God. Marriage perhaps comes closest to describe such a union and yet even that fails to express the oneness of persons, Trinity and ourselves individually and all of us together united in the Eucharist.

M.V. Bernadot, O.P., by means of analogies, strives to describe the intimacy of the communicant and God in this Eucharistic union, but such analogies always fail to throw adequate light on this mystery.

As perfume percolates the containing vessel, and the ray the crystal, giving purity and brilliance; like fire permeating iron, warming and enkindling, so Grace from the Eucharist flowing into my soul, possesses, penetrates, fills, in the words of St. Thomas "transforms and inebriates with God."[11]

Because Jesus Christ through His Spirit takes us up, not only into His human nature but into His very divine nature, we are more than adopted children. We can say with St. John: "Think of the love that the Father has lavished on us, by letting us be called God's children; and that is what we are. My dear people, we are already the children of God . . ." (1 Jn 3:1-2). We in the Eucharist experience ourselves more deeply being regenerated by the Father into a oneness with Jesus Christ as His Son. Scheeben is one of the boldest of modern theologians to express this substantial union with Christ received in the Eucharist:

In the Eucharist we receive life from God; and we receive it by substantial union with His Son, inasmuch as we become bone of His bone and flesh of His flesh. Indeed, our substantial connection with Him is more enduring than that which exists among men between parent and child. For in this latter case the substantial union ceases with birth; but in the Eucharist it can and should be continually renewed and strengthened. And so in virtue of the Eucharist we not merely receive our life from God, as children do from their earthly parents, but we live in God; we have our life from His substance and in His substance. Eucharistic Communion with God has the double function of begetting and nourishing the children of God.[12]

ONE WITH EACH OTHER

In the Eucharist we are not only united with the Trinity but we attain a new oneness with the others in whom the same trinitarian life lives, especially within the context of the Eucharistic celebration. Here is where the Church, the Body of Christ, comes together in loving union with its Head, Jesus Christ. The Liturgy or the "work" of the People of God has to be always the context (except in emergencies such as Communion given to the sick) in which the Eucharist is received. The Liturgy is the sacred place and time when the Church is most realized by the power of the Holy Spirit. It is the realization of the life of the Church for which it exists: to praise and glorify God for the gifts of life and salvation we have received.

It is especially in the reception of the Eucharist that all members of Christ's Body are most powerfully united in a new sense of oneness with each other. They symbolically enter into the depths of the richness of God's self-sacrificing love. The Eucharist is not only a sacrament but it is also the ever-now sacrifice of Christ for us to the Father unto our healing and redemption. It is the culmination of all the sacraments as encounters with Christ in His self-giving to us, for in the Eucharist Jesus Christ gives Himself as He did in the first Eucharistic celebration of the Last Supper before His death and as He did on the cross.

He gives Himself solemnly to die on our behalf, ratifying by this visible, external ritual act the whole meaning and basic choice of His earthly life. "Now has the Son of Man been glorified, and in him God has been glorified" (Jn 13:21).

All of Christ's other powerful miracles and healings have meaning in the light of this greatest power of communication whereby He gives Himself to us in the complete gift. He not merely expresses His desire to die for us individually and communally for the whole of mankind, but He gives us His body as food and His blood as drink. He finds a way to remain among us, imaging always the sacrificing love of the Father unto the last drop of water and blood for us.

In making the first Covenant, Yahweh had promised to be faithful to His people if they would faithfully observe the Torah. He also showed Himself the patient, tender spouse of Israel. Jesus renews this tender, spousal love of God for His people. The Eucharist is the banquet and Jesus is the Bridegroom. The Church, made up of the community of individual believers in Him, is the Bride. Lives are to be changed. Abiding in the Eucharistic union with the Father and the Son, we are to bring forth fruit in abundance. "It is to the glory of my Father that you should bear much fruit, and then you will be my disciples. . . . Remain in my love. If you keep my commandments, you will remain in my love. This is my commandment: love one another as I have loved you" (Jn 15:8-12).

The divinizing power of the Trinity experienced in the Eucharist is to be the power that drives us outward towards other communities to be Eucharist, bread broken, to give ourselves not only as Jesus did on our behalf, but with

Jesus and the Father abiding within us with their Spirit of
love empowering us to do that which would be impossible
for us alone to do consistently. St. Paul sees immediately
the application of the Eucharist-community to the Christian family. "Husbands should love their wives just as
Christ loved the Church and sacrificed himself for her to
make her holy" (Ep 5:25).

The sacrifice of Jesus Christ acted out in the
Eucharistic Liturgy is unto the remission of our sins. This
is not a legalistic *quid pro quo* contract to satisfy the demands of divine justice. The blood of Jesus that remits our
sins and heals us unto eternal life is to be a daily experience
of the depths of God's love manifested for us by Jesus'
complete self-giving. His ardent love, experienced in the
Eucharist, is a reliving of the same dynamic, *ever-now* love
of Jesus, God-man, for us as He touches us with both His
humanity and divinity and takes away the condition of sin
in our lives. Loved so madly by God the Father, Son and
Holy Spirit, we need no longer resort to sinful actions,
words and thoughts that are ego-centered and destructive
of community oneness. We can, by the power of the Holy
Spirit, who reveals to us, within these symbols of food and
drink, the presence of the loving Trinity, let go of our lives
and live and love as God does.

The Church, as a community of one Body united in
love to the one Head, Jesus Christ, is formed out of the
womb of Christ's heart that is an image of the heart of the
Father. Water and blood, two elements that St. John sees
at the foot of the cross (Jn 19:34) are to be symbols of the
creative forces of the female, symbols of the life-giving
power that Jesus, dying on the cross, gives to His Bride,
the Church, signs of the birth-giving waters of Baptism

and the nourishing Body and Blood of Christ in the Eucharist. St. John Chrysostom comments on the wounded side of Christ:

> The lance of the soldier opened the side of Christ, and behold . . . from his wounded side Christ built the Church, as once the first mother, Eve, was formed from Adam. Hence Paul says: Of his flesh we are and of his bone. By that he means the wounded side of Jesus. As God took the rib out of Adam's side and from it formed the woman, so Christ gives us water and blood from his wounded side and forms from it the Church . . . there the slumber of Adam; here the death-sleep of Jesus.[13]

We are born spiritually as God's children, brothers and sisters to each other as we truly live the sacrament of Baptism that reaches its fullness of loving union between us and God and between one another of us human brothers and sisters in the Eucharist. In the Old Covenant the blood of goats and bulls and the ashes of heifers were sprinkled on those who incurred defilement and they were restored to the holiness of their outward lives. "How much more effectively the blood of Christ, who offered himself as the perfect sacrifice to God through the eternal Spirit, can purify our inner self from dead actions so that we do our service to the living God" (Heb 9:13-14).

SELF-SACRIFICE

Through His humanity, His body and blood, Jesus Christ is the victim, but in the Eucharist we also receive the only existing Jesus Christ, glorified and spiritualized by the victory of resurrection over sin and death. We are to draw strength from this sacrifice to stir us also to sacrifice ourselves for each other. We are to participate in Christ's sacrifice by offering ourselves not only to God but concretely we are to be consumed by the fire of love of God in Jesus Christ through His Spirit to go forth and be a living sacrifice of love to all that we meet.

The principal fruit of the Eucharist, "the communion in the Holy Spirit," is an intimate union of all men in the Mystical Body of Christ. We find in the *epiklesis* of St. Basil's Liturgy the stress on this union: "So that all who participate from one bread may be made one by the action of the One Spirit." This is the central scope of the Eucharist, the union of all the faithful through the mutual union of each individual with the Holy Trinity. The Eucharist creates the unity of all who participate in the same holy bread.

This comes through a single effusion of the Holy Spirit in all of the communicants who receive the Bread of life with sincerity and fervor. St. Paul tells us that it is the Holy Spirit who pours out gifts in order to "edify" or build up the Body of Christ, the Church. "There is a variety of gifts but always the same Spirit; there are all sorts of service to be done, but always to the same Lord . . ." (1 Co 12:4-5). Again St. Paul writes: "There is one Body, one Spirit, just as you were all called into one and the same hope when you were called. There is one Lord, one faith, one Baptism, and one God who is Father of all, over all, through all and within all" (Ep 4:4-6).

Therefore, we not only receive Jesus Christ in the Eucharist in order to praise God the Father and surrender ourselves to Him in the same self-surrendering act of Jesus

Christ on the cross, but we are to be transformed interiorly by Christ's Spirit. "Be renewed in the spirit of your mind" (Ep 4:23). By praising and glorifying the Heavenly Father, we open ourselves in the Eucharist and at all times after the Eucharist to His transforming blessing that He breathes upon us to make us a true, effective, Eucharistic blessing to all whom we meet.

We put on the mind of Christ in the Eucharist when we face with Him a broken, suffering world. We become a living part of the Body of Christ, we become Church when we share the caring love of Jesus for each suffering person we meet. Pain gnaws at our hearts as we suffer the pain of the heart of Christ not to be able to do more for the poor and afflicted in all parts of the world. We suffer in our own inadequacies that do not allow us to know what we can effectively do to alleviate the physical and moral evils rampant in the world.

With St. Paul we can ask whether we have received Christ's Body in the Eucharist if, after the liturgical celebration, we do not receive as a brother or sister of our one Father, each human being who enters our life.

> . . . and so anyone who eats the bread or drinks the cup of the Lord unworthy will be behaving unworthily towards the body and blood of the Lord . . . because a person who eats and drinks without recognizing the Body is eating and drinking his own condemnation (1 Co 11:27-29).

St. Paul was speaking about sins against charity toward fellow Christians. He had earlier in the same epistle commented on the oneness that true reception of the Body of Jesus Christ effects. "The fact that there is only one loaf means that, though there are many of us, we form a single body, because we all have a share in this one loaf'' (1 Co 10:17). The Eucharist is not fully received unless it is lived. And the living Eucharist is our daily life in Jesus Christ where we live no longer we are ourselves but He truly lives in us (Ga 2:20).

We are to go out and to be Eucharist to every man, woman and child that God sends into our lives. What a tremendous responsibility for Christians who believe the doctrine of the Eucharist and receive this Gift of gifts even daily! Our Eucharistic life is to be measured by the fruit of the Spirit that is love, peace, joy, gentleness, kindliness, patience and forbearance (Ga 5:22). We are to ''bear with one another charitably, in complete selflessness, gentleness and patience. Do all you can to preserve the unity of the Spirit by the peace that binds you together'' (Ep 4:2).

We are to use our special charisms or gifts given us by the Holy Spirit to build up the Body of Christ. If one part of the Body of Christ is wounded or sick, the healthy parts come to the aid of the injured member. But the greatest sign of whether we have truly received the full Body of Christ is measured by love for this is the indication of how much of God's Eucharistic love has been received in receiving the body and blood of Jesus Christ, the image of the Father. Such love is toward others as Jesus, the imaged love of the Father, was always toward others in loving service. ''If I, then, the Lord and Master, have washed your feet, you should wash each other's feet'' (Jn 13:14). This Eucharistic love is always patient and kind, never jealous, never boastful or conceited, never rude or selfish. It does not take offense and is not resentful. It takes no pleasure in other people's sins but delights in the truth. It is always ready to excuse, to trust, to hope and to endure whatever comes (1 Co 13:4-6).

THE COSMIC EUCHARIST

The fruit of the Eucharist as the gift of the Holy Spirit unifying us who have received Jesus Christ in love with all mankind is beautifully described by Teilhard de Chardin:

The gift you ask of me for these brothers of mine—the only gift my heart can give—is not the overflowing tenderness of those special, preferential loves which you implant in our lives as the most powerful created agent of our inward growth; it is something less tender but just as real and of even greater strength. Your will is that, with the help of your Eucharist, between men and my brother-men there should be revealed that basic attraction (already dimly felt in every love once it becomes strong) which mystically transforms the myriads of rational creatures into (as it were) a single monad in you, Christ Jesus.[14]

Jesus, the Risen Lord over all the universe, the *Pantocrator,* by His resurrection is inserted as a leaven inside of the entire, material cosmos. Yet He operates, He speaks, He touches, He loves the poor and the destitute, He conquers sin and death empirically only through His living members. Those who worthily have received His body and blood and have received the outpoured Holy Spirit in the Eucharist are to go out and celebrate the Eucharistic Liturgy of the High-Priest, Jesus Christ.

God truly loves the world He created. He looked upon it and saw it to be very good (Gn 1:18). He has created all things, every atom of matter, in and through His Word, Jesus Christ. We are to go forth from the altar of the Lord to witness to the sustaining presence of God's Logos, not only living within us but also sustaining all of creation. Having received the Trinity and having been divinized into their very community of one in unity and many in self-giving relationships, we are to go forth and draw out these energies of the same Trinity that bathe the whole universe and charge it with God's infinite love.

The Body of Christ is being formed through the Eucharistic ministry of each human being made according to that Image and Likeness that is Jesus Christ. That Body of Christ is being shaped and fashioned by all things material. There are prophets of doom who point out the chaotic confusion and dogmatically declare as Sartre that life has "no exit." Nevertheless Christians, who have eaten the Bread of Life, point to the inner, loving presence of the Cosmic Christ within matter, within this crazy, careening world. They show that there is a divine purpose, similar to the purpose revealed to them as they reverently received the glorified humanity of Jesus Christ. The same Holy Spirit that swept them and their fellow communicants into a realized oneness with Jesus Christ and His Father reveals to them at each step of their daily lives how to effect that same union with the world. The Spirit reveals the inner presence, now being activated in time and place by the persons in whom Jesus Christ lives, of that same Jesus Christ as He evolves the universe into His Body. He is moving it towards Omega which he is. "I am the Alpha and the Omega, says the Lord God, who is, who was, and who is to come, the Almighty" (Rv 1:8).

Such "Eucharized" Christians live in the vision of the dynamic love energies inside of the material world. They can call other people to their awesome dignity of co-operating with these uncreated energies of God. Creation is not finished. The Cosmic Liturgy has not yet reached communion, men and women, united with each other as

brothers and sisters of Jesus Christ and of the one Heavenly Father, human beings in peace and harmony with the
sub-human cosmos, bringing it into fulfillment according
to God's eternal plan. They have entered through the
Eucharist into a life in Christ, a new creation. The old
creation for them has gone, and now the new one is here.

> It is all God's Work. It was God who reconciled us to
> himself through Christ and gave us the work of handing on
> this reconciliation. In other words, God in Christ was
> reconciling the world to himself, not holding men's faults
> against them, and he has entrusted to us the news that they
> are reconciled (2 Co 5:18-19).

As men and women work, ever more conscious of the
indwelling Trinity brought to such a peak of experience in
the Eucharist, they join the gifts of creativity placed within
them by God's graces with the working power of the triune
God, Father, Son and Holy Spirit. In humility they can
also see the pruning hand of God, the Divine Pedagogue,
as He instructs His children, corrects, admonishes, exhorts
them in what seems to be, at times, sheer negative evil,
physical or moral, for those not in the Body of Christ.

They live each moment in the resurrectional hope that
is engendered in the social and historical horizontal. Instead of running away from involvement in the activities of
this world, such Christians move to the "inside" presence
of the Trinity at the heart of matter. What any human being adds to make this world a better world in Christ Jesus
has an eternal effect on the whole process. When the love
experienced in the Eucharist becomes the dominant force
in the lives of such Christians, then every thought, word

and deed is bathed in the light of the indwelling Trinity inside the whole world.

Thus the building up of the Body of Christ, the Church, is not the gathering of an elite group out of the human race, while the rest of creation is destined for destruction. It is to be the resurrected body of God's creation, evolving through history and brought to its completion with man's cooperation. The only obstacles that hold back the process are the same that do not allow us truly to receive the Body of Christ fully in the Eucharist: the evils of selfishness, fear and pride.

CONCLUSION

In his introduction to the works of William Blake, the poet Yeats wrote: "We perceive the world through countless little reflections of our own image."[15] We spend most of our lives creating the world according to our own needs. Religious leaders often easily help in this process as they encourage their "faithful" to build their own world and in that man-created world they are to know that they have been saved. But the entire Christian revelation consists in the power of Jesus Christ as light, coming into our darkened world, and leading us through His Spirit to the Source of all reality, the Heavenly Father.

He is the Image of the Father and we have been made according to His likeness (Gn 1:26). Jesus Christ has taken upon Himself our human nature in order to set us free from our illusions and false worlds. He came to reveal that all reality, all of our created world, has come out of the family of God, a tri-unity of three Persons in one nature. Creation is an on-going presence of God as one energizing love, touching our world with three personalized relations of Fatherhood, Sonship and Spiration of love.

This Unity in Trinity, the motionless movement of God toward His world as the receptacle of His love, becomes manifested to us when God's Logos, the Son of the Father, assumed flesh in the mystery of the Incarnation. Now through the humanity of Jesus Christ God the Trinity touches us and our material world through us. Through His death and resurrection, Jesus Christ is able to send to us God's Spirit. It is in the Eucharist, as we have seen, that we reach the climax of these two mysteries that bring us into true reality, that of the Trinity and the Incarnation.

We are called to live in this reality of the all-pervasive, loving presence of the Trinity acting through the mediation of the God-Man, Jesus Christ. This is what a Christian mystic really is. As he celebrates the Divine Liturgy, his faith makes him vividly aware of this trinitarian presence, when, in microcosmic fashion, Jesus the High-Priest breathes over a small segment of the Church, including their gifts of bread and wine, and His Spirit of love transfigures this part of the incomplete world into a sharing in Christ's divine nature. The authentic Christian mystic extends this transfiguring Liturgy throughout his day in every thought, word and deed, done for God's glory. No matter how insignificant, banal and monotonous his work may be he is vibrantly aware of Jesus Christ, already glorified, living within him and working through him to bring the whole world to its fullness.

As communion with the body and blood of Jesus Christ brings the contemplative Christian into the dynamic presence of the Trinity, so this communion with Him is extended into the materiality of each day. The false division between the profane and the sacred ceases as he prayerfully contemplates the Holy Trinity in all of creation. Contemplation flows from the fullness of his activities, because he finds the Trinity in the very activity of the moment. He discovers the divine richness in the most commonplace action. He finds the Holy Trinity at work for the redemption of the human race and he becomes an instrument of applying that divine, healing love to each person he meets. He has new "eyes" with which to see, not only the uncreated energies of the one God, essentially working out of love, but to see also and to experience the Divine Father becoming His Father and the Father of all his brothers and sisters. He sees the Son not only always adoring the Father in total self-surrendering love but he sees Him also as his Head, while he is a part, a member of His total, complete Body. He experiences the loving presence of the Spirit, not only binding the Father and Son into a oneness that calls out their uniqueness of person, but also binding himself and all other human beings and the whole material universe into a oneness of the Body of Christ with a uniqueness assigned to each individual human person and each material creature.

For such a contemplative, there is no insignificant event that does not bear the stamp of the Holy Trinity's actively involved, loving presence, touching the world through the humanity of Jesus Christ, now joined to that of the man of prayer in order to bring it to completion according to the original plan as conceived by the Holy Trinity. Such a contemplative patiently lives day by day in the mystery of the Trinity's presence in his life. He shuns any objectivizing of this awesome mystery of God as one and God as three loving relationships to each other and to himself.

He is a humble pilgrim, always searching deeper into reality that is permeated by the triune presence of Father, Son and Holy Spirit. He cries out for pardon and cleansing: "Lord, Jesus Christ, Son of God, have mercy on me a sinner!" He approaches each moment as he does the moment in the Divine Liturgy when he is about to receive the Fiery Coal of Divine Love in the Eucharist: "Approach with faith and in the fear of God." The mystery of the Trinity does not mean that we cannot experience the reality of God's loving *We*-community. It means that such knowledge is beyond our human acquisition, but it is given to those who hunger and thirst for it. St. Paul believed that such knowledge was available to the poor of spirit:

> Out of his infinite glory, may he give you the power through his Spirit for your hidden self to grow strong, so that Christ may live in your hearts through faith, and then, planted in love and built on love, you will with all the saints have strength to grasp the breadth and the length, the height and the depth; until, knowing the love of Christ, which is beyond all knowledge, you are filled with the utter fullness of God (Ep 3:16-19).

God is a fullness, an inexhaustible source of love that seeks continuously to share His very being with us human beings. But He seeks to reveal Himself as Trinity and as One to those who move beyond the type of *religion* that allows us to fashion our own images of God and the world and of others after our own image. To the little ones of this earth, the poor of spirit and clean of heart, God reveals through His Holy Spirit how simple bread and wine can open us up to the living Bread of life, Jesus Christ, true God and true man. The Eucharistic Lord leads us to the ever-present Father of both Jesus Christ and of ourselves who through the Eucharist have become united one with the only begotten Son of God. Through the Eucharist such little ones move into the world and find the presence of the risen Jesus not only in bread and wine but in the little pebble, the smile of a child, the sparkle in the wise eyes of an old man. The whole world is a part of the eternal Liturgy that the Lamb of God is offering to the Heavenly Father. The heart of all reality is Eucharist: receiving God's so great love for us in His Son incarnated, Jesus Christ, through the illumination of the Holy Spirit who empowers us to return that love in self-surrendering service to each person we meet. The Trinity is at the beginning of all reality and it is there that we end up in humble adoration.

T.S. Eliot, in his Four Quartets, well describes our search for the utter fullness of God:

> We shall not cease from exploration,
> And the end of all our exploring
> Will be to arrive where we started
> And know the place for the first time.[16]

A fitting conclusion to such a book for an author who has striven to present the apophatic side of the mystery of the Trinity and yet has succeeded in the process to write so many pages are the words of St. Symeon the New Theologian (+1022) who will recall us to this awesome mystery that can be perceived only by the humble and meek of heart.

> So then come and place yourself with us, O my brother,
> on the mountain of divine knowledge of divine contemplation

and together let us hear the Father's voice—O alas!
How far are we from the divine dignity!
How far away are we from eternal life!
How far or even farther are we all, really,
from the dignity of God and divine contemplation,
even if we should affirm in a contradictory way that we
    abide in Him
and we possess in us Him who abides in unapproach-
    able light,
who also entirely remains and abides in us,
and yet we would wish, seated in the bowels of the
    earth,
to philosophize on things that transcend this earth,
on things of Heaven and even higher things than that,
    as though we saw reality accurately,
and so we seek to explain to everyone and enjoy being
    called learned men,
theologians, experts and mystics of divine secrets
which just proves completely our stupidity.
. . . But, O my Christ, deliver those who are tied to You
from the unclean vanity and pride.
Make us participators in Your sufferings and Your glory
and deign to make us never to be separated from You,
now and in the future world to come,
forever and ever. Amen.[17]

FIRE FLY

Fire fly, dancing in the dark,
what makes you glow so?
O *Phosphoros,* Light-bearer,
Is it because the light of Christ
    shines in you, through you
    to lighten up the darkness?

Why is there light,
    and then the silent darkness
    soon broken by soft light?
Why not total light
    all the time
    dispelling all the night's darkness?

O Christ, be the light,
Phos Hilaron, Radiant Light,
    that I may carry
    into the world's darkness.
Make me a carrier of your light,
    that I may be
    flashing light across the night.

In the night I stretch out
    to embrace your light.
Come, Bright Light of love,
    phosphorize my being!
May your light be total,
    not on or off,
    but may it consume
    the darkness in me.

Fire fly, flash away in the night.
For full day soon will be here.
And no one will see your light
    until there returns again the night.

O Christ, be full noon to me!
Or if night must be,
May your light be constant,
    not flashing, off and on.
May I carry your light
    be your light to others
    who sleep in the dark of night.

Rev. George Maloney, S.J.

FOOTNOTES

Chapter One

1. For a penetrating, Jungian development of this myth, cf.: Robert A. Johnson: *He-Understanding Masculine Psychology* (N.Y. Perennial Library, Harper & Row, 1974).

2. St. Augustine: *Confessiones;* X, 27, 38; *PL* XXXII, 795.

3. Emil Brunner: *Man in Revolt* (London, 1953) p. 97.

4. St. Gregory of Nyssa: *Life of Moses,* tr. A.J. Malherbe and E. Ferguson (N.Y.: Paulist Press, 1978) in the Series: *The Classics of Western Spirituality,* no. 226, p. 113.

5. G. Maloney: *Inward Stillness* (Denville, N.J.: Dimension Books, 1976) pp. 87-88.

6. St. Gregory of Sinai: *Instructions to Hesychasts,* in: *Writings from the Philokalia on Prayer of the Heart,* tr. E. Kaloubovsky and G.E.H. Palmer (London: Faber & Faber, 1951), p. 84.

7. St. Irenaeus: *Adversus Haereses,* in: *The Ante-Nicene Fathers,* Vol. 1; ed. A. Roberts and J. Donaldson (Grand Rapids, Mich.), Bk 111, ch. 19, 1, pp. 448-449. cf. also: 111, ch. 10, 2, p. 424; IV, ch. 33, 4, p. 507; IV, ch. 38, 4, p. 552; IV. Ch. 39, 2, p. 523.

8. St. Augustine: *De Trinitate,* V, 1, 2; PL XLII, 912.

9. Cited by C. Butler: *Western Mysticism* (London, 1927) pp. 270-271.

10.   Evelyn Underhill: *The School of Charity and the Mystery of Sacrifice* (N.Y.: Longmans, Green and Co., 1956) p. 235.

11.   Pseudo-Dionysius: *Mystical Theology,* 1.

12.   Cf.: A. Tanquerey: *The Spiritual Life: A Treatise on Ascetical and Mystical Theology* (Newman: Westminster, Md., 1947).

13.   On this topic cf.: William Johnston: *The Still Point* (N.Y.: Fordham Univ. Press, 1970)

14.   Karl Rahner: *Encyclopedia of Theology* (London: Burns and Oates, 1975), p. 1010.

15.   M. Raymond: "Mystical Life-Mystical Prayer" in: *Review for Religious,* 8 (1949) pp. 123-126. Cf. also: Felix Podimattam: "The Universal Call to Mysticism," in: *Jeevadhara,* 42 (Nov-Dec., 1977, Kottayam, Kerala, India) pp. 471-497.

16.   St. Irenaeus: *Adversus Haereses,* op. cit. IV, Ch. 11, 2, p. 474.

17.   This formed the theme of my book: *Inscape: God at the Heart of Matter* (Denville, N.J.: Dimension Books, 1978).

18.   Cf.: G. Maloney, S.J.: *A Theology of Uncreated Energies* (Milwaukee: Marquette Univ. Press, 1978).

19.   Mother Teresa: "The Poor in Our Midst," in: *New Covenant* (Ann Arbor, Mich, Jan. 1977) cited by Wm. Johnston: *The Inner Eye of Love* (London: Collins, 1978) p. 26-27.

20.   St. Symeon the New Theologian: *Hymn* 12, 9-25, in: *Hymns of Divine Love,* tr. by G.A. Maloney, S.J. (Denville, N.J.: Dimension Books, 1975) p. 39.

21.   Ibid, *Hymn* 52, op. cit., pp. 264-265.

Chapter Two

1.   Karl Rahner: *The Trinity* (N.Y.: Herder & Herder, 1969) tr. J. Donceel, S.J. pp. 10-11.

2.   Raimundo Panikkar: *The Trinity and the Religious Experience of Man* (N.Y.: Orbis Books, 1973).

3.   K. Rahner, op. cit., p. 99.

4.   M.J. Scheeben: *The Mysteries of Christianity* (St. Louis: B. Herder Bk. Co., 1946) tr. Cyril Vollert, S.J., p. 48.

5.   K. Rahner, op. cit., takes to task St. Augustine and those theologians who have followed his opinion that any one of the three Persons within the Trinity could have become incarnate if God should so have wished. Cf.: pp. 11; 73 ss; 103 ss.).

6.   M. Scheeben, op. cit., p. 445.

7.   Cf.: V. Lossky: *The Mystical Theology of the Eastern Church* (Cambridge & London: James Clarke & Co. Ltd., 1957) p. 71.

8.   K. Rahner, op. cit., p. 22.

9.   Ibid., p. 101.

10. Roland D. Zimany: "Grace, Deification and Sanctification: East-West, in: *Diakonia* 12 (1977) p. 125. For a complete treatment of the energies of God cf.: G. Maloney, S.J.: *A Theology of Uncreated Energies* (Milwaukee: Marquette Univ. Press, 1978).

11. Several modern theologians have been writing articles that present the Trinity and man's relationships as interpersonal. Cf.: E. Cousins: "A Theology of Interpersonal Relations," in: *Thought* 45 (1970) 56-82; J. Brocken: "The Holy Trinity as a Community of Divine Persons," in: *Heythrop Journal* 15 (1974) pp. 166-182; 257-270; T. O'Connell: "Grace, Relationship and Transcendental Analysis," in: *Thought* 48 (1973) pp. 360-385 and P. Fransen: *The New Life of Grace* (N.Y. Sheed & Ward, 1972) pp. 52-59.

12. V. Lossky: "Apophasis and Trinitarian Theology," in: *In the Image and Likeness of God* (N.Y.: St. Vladimir's Seminary Press, 1974).

13. St. John Damascene: *De Fide Orthodoxa;* Bk. 50; 4; PG 94, 800 B.

Chapter Three

1. St. Cyril of Alexandria in his first discourse against Julian the Apostate, PG 76, 532-533 and St. Ambrose of Milan in: *De Excessu Fratris sui satyri,* Lib. 11; Pl 16, 1342, both write of the scene of Abraham and the apparition of the three angels as an image of the Trinity.

2. This famous icon can still be seen today in the Tretiakov Gallery in Moscow.

3. It was forbidden in the Council of Trullo (686 A.D.) to paint any icon depicting the Father as a human being with a beard.

4. Pseudo-Dionysius: *On Divine Names;* PG 3, 916 D.

5. *Meister Eckhart,* ed. Franz Pfeiffer, 2 vols., tr. C. de B. Evans (London: Watkins, 1947): Sermon LVIII, *Divine Understanding,* p. 148.

6. Th. De Regnon, S.J.: *Etudes de la th9ologie positive sur la Sainte Trinit9* (Paris, 1892-98) vol. 1, p. 433.

7. V. Lossky: *The Mystical Theology of the Eastern Church* (Cambridge and London: James Clarke & Co. Ltd., 1957) p. 56.

8. St. Gregory Nazianzus: *Homilia XLII,* 15; PG 36, 476.

9. Pseudo-Dionysius: *The Divine Names and the Mystical Theology,* tr. C.E. Rolt (London: SPCK, 1920), DN 11, 4, p. 69.

10. R. Panikkar, op. cit. pp. 46-47.

11. Meister Eckhart, op. cit., p. 267.

12. Thomas Merton: *Cables to the Ace or Familiar Liturgies of Misunderstanding* (N.Y.: New Directions, 1967) p. 58.

13. Dr. Carl Rogers: *On Becoming a Person* (Boston: Houghton Mifflin Co., 1961) p. 90.

14. Cited by Archbishop Anthony Bloom: *Meditations.* Dimension Books, (Denville, N.J., 1972) p. 9.

15. Rudolf Otto: *Mysticism East and West;* tr. B. Bracey and R. Payne, 1932, p. 151.

16. St. Augustine: The Trinity, tr. Stephen McKenna, C.SS.R. in *The Fathers of the Church Series,* vol. 45 (Wash. D.C.: The Catholic Univ. Press, 1963) Bk. V, ch. 11, p. 189.

17. Ibid., Bk. VII, ch. 4, p. 229.

18. St. Hilary of Poitiers: *The Trinity,* tr. Stephen McKenna, C.SS.R. in *The Fathers of the Church Series,* vol. 25 (Wash. D.C.: Catholic Univ. Press, 1954) Bl. 2, 6; p. 41.

19. R. Panikkar, op. cit., p. 46.

20. Gerald Vann, O.P.: *The Pain of Christ and the Sorrow of God* (London: Blackfriars, 1947) p. 69. On the *pathos* of God, cf.: Robert Wild: *Who I Will be—Is There Joy and Suffering in God?* (Denville, N.J.: Dimension Bks., 1976); J. Moltmann: *The Crucified God* (London: SCM Press, Ltd., 1974) pp. 271-276; A.J. Heschel: *The Prophets* (N.Y.: Harper & Row, 1971) vol. 11, ch. 1, "The Theology of Pathos."

Chapter Four

1. St. Augustine: *City of God:* XI, 26. in: Fathers of the Church Series; tr. G. Walsh, S.J. and Sr. Grace Monahan, OSV (N.Y.: Fathers of the Church, Inc., 1952) p. 228.

2. K. Rahner, op. cit., p. 35.

3. H. Mühlen: *Der Heilige Geist als Person* (Münster: Aschendorff, 1966).

4. Richard of St. Victor: *De Trinitate:* Bk. III, c. 19; PL 196; 915B-930D.

5. E. Gilson: *The Mystical Theology of St. Bernard* (N.Y.; Sheed & Ward, 1940), p. 120.

6. St. Ignatius of Antioch: *Letter to the Magnesians;* VIII, 2. *PGV,* 765.

7. On the Greek paideia, see: Werner Jaeger: *Early Christianity and Greek Paideia* (Cambridge: Cambridge Univ. Press, 1961).

8. C.T. Wood: *The Life, Letters and Religion of St. Paul* (Edinburgh, 1925) p. 320.

9. St. Athanasius: De Decretis, 27, in: A Select Library of Nicene and Post-Nicene Fathers of the Christian Church, 2nd Series; 3d. Philip Schaff and Henry Wace, Vol. 4: St. Athanasius, Select Works and Letters (Grand Rapids, Mich.: Eerdmans, 1957), abbrev. LNPF, p. 168.

10. St. Athanasius: *De Incarnatione,* 54; LNPF, op. cit., p. 65.

11. Richard of St. Victor: *De Trinitate,* 3, 2, ed. Jean Ribaillier, pp. 136-137.

12. Ibid., p. 138.

13. Ibid., p. 147.

14. I have used in this book many insights given by Mühlen in his main work: *Der Heilige Geist als Person* (2nd ed.; Münster: Aschendorff, 1966), abbrev. hereafter as *GP.* The insights of Robert Sears, S.J. in his unpublished doctoral thesis have also been used.

15. Dietrich von Hildebrand: *Metaphysik der Gemeinschaft* (Regensberg: J. Habbel, 1955).

16. Wilhelm von Humboldt: *Gesammelte Schriften,* hrsg. v.d. Preuss. *Akademie d. Wissenschaften* (17 vols.; Berlin: B. Beher's Verlag, 1903-1936).

17. Cf.: Dale Moody: *Spirit of the Living God* (Philadelphia: The Westminster Press, 1968) pp. 33-57.

18. Cf.: Hendrikus Berkhof: *The Doctrine of the Holy Spirit* (Richmond, Va.: John Knox Press, 1964) p. 27.

19. Wilhelm von Humboldt: op. cit., art.: "Uber die Verwandtschaft der Ortsadverbien mit dem Pronomen in einigen Sprachen," p. 304f.

20. Dietrich von Hildebrand: op. cit., p. 34.

21. Saint Bonaventure: *The Mind's Road to God,* tr. G. Boas (Indianapolis: Bobbs-Merrill, 1953) ch. V, pp. 34, 35, 39.

Chapter Five

1. Gerard Manley Hopkins: *God's Grandeur.*

2. St. Irenaeus: *Adversus Haereses:* Bk. V, ch. 28,4, *ANF (The Ante-Nicene Fathers* Vol. 1, ed. A. Roberts and J. Donaldson (Grand Rapids: Eerdmans, 1958) p. 557.

3. cf.: G. Maloney, S.J.: *A Theology of Uncreated Energies* (Milwaukee: Marquette Univ. Press, 1978).

4. St. Basil of Caesarea: *Epistola 234;* PG XXX11, 869.

5. St. Thomas: *Summa Theologiae,* la 2ae, Q.109, intro., 2 ans.Q.110,1 ans.

6. St. Augustine: *De Trinitate,* Bk. 5,8-9.

7. cf.: John Chethimattam, C.M.I., *Consciousness and Reality* (Bangalore: Bangalore Press, 1967) pp. 233-40; also: Ewert Cousins: "Trinity and World Religions," in: *Journal of Ecumenical Studies,* Vol. 7, no. 3 (1970) pp. 476-498.

8. St. Bonaventure: *Quaestiones Disputatae de Mysterio Trinitatis,* 1 sent., d.3, p.l, a.un., q.4.

9. St. Gregory Palamas: *Capita Physica,* 68, *PG* 150, 1169.

10. cf.: G. Maloney, S.J.: The Cosmic Christ from Paul to Teilhard (N.Y.: Sheed & Ward, 1968); R. Hale: *Christ and the Universe. Teilhard de Chardin and the Cosmos* (Chicago: Franciscan Press, 1973).

11. M. Schmaus: *Katolische Dogmatik* (München; 1963) 11, 2, p. 461.

12. St. Maximus the Confessor: *Quaestiones ad Thalassium,* 21; PG 90, 312-316.

13. St. Maximus the Confessor: *Epistola XXI;* PG 91,604 BC.

14. St. Athanasius: *De Incarnatione Verbi;* PG 25,192B.

15. St. Cyril of Alexandria: *De recta Fide ad Theodosium;* PG 76,1177 A.

16. S. Bulgakov: *Paraclet* (Paris, 1946) pp. 268, 270.

17. P. Evdokimov: "L'Esprit Saint et l'Eglise d'après la tradition liturgique," in: *L'Esprit Saint et l'Eglise.* Actes du Symposium organisé par l'Académie Internationale des Sciences Religieuses (Paris, 1969) p. 92.

18. S. Bulgakov, op. cit., pp. 145, 164, 174 f.

19. Thomas Hopko: "Holy Spirit in Orthodox Theology and Life," in: *Commonweal* (Nov. 8, 1968), Vol. LXXXIX, no. 6, p. 187.

20. Teilhard de Chardin: "Super-Humanité, Super-Christ, Super-Charité," in: *Oeuvres de Pierre Teilhard de Chardin:* Vol. 9: Science et Christ (Paris: Editions du Seuil, 1965) p. 213.

21. For further development of this theme, cf.: G. Maloney: *Inscape: God at the Heart of Matter* (Denville, N.J.: Dimension Bks., 1978).

22. Julian of Norwich: *Showings;* tr. E. Colledge and J. Walsh, in: *The Classics of Western Spirituality* (N.Y.— Ramsey, N.J.: Paulist Press, 1978) p. 183.

23. R.A. Errico: *The Lord's Prayer* (San Antonio: Aramaic Bible Center, Inc., 1975) p. 13.

24. Louis de Blois, quoted by H.A. Reinhold: *The Soul Afire* (Garden City, N.Y.: Image Bks. Doubleday & Co., 1973) p. 358-359.

25. Teilhard de Chardin: *Le Milieu Mystique,* as found in Pensée 80, in: *Hymn of the Universe* (N.Y.: Harper Torchbooks, 1965) p. 154.

Chapter Six

1. William Shakespeare: *As you Like It,* in: *The Complete Works,* ed. G.B. Harrison (N.Y.: Harcourt, Brace & Co., 1948) Vol. 11, pp. 142-143.

2. Carl G. Jung: *The Basic Writings,* ed. Violet Staub de Laszlo (N.Y.: Pantheon Books, Inc., 1959) p. 143.

3. William Butler Yeats: "Life," in: *The Variorum Edition of the Poems of W.B. Yeats,* ed. Peter Allt and Russell K. Alspach (N.Y.: The Macmillan Co., 1957).

4. Ibid.: "Vacillation."

5. Hermann Hesse: *Steppenwolf;* tr. Basil Creighton (N.Y.: Henry Holt and Co., 1928) p. 78.

6. M. Scheeben: op. cit., pp. 445-446.

7. St. Maximus the Confessor: *Centuria* 1, 8-13; *PG* 90, 1182-1186.

8. St. Symeon the New Theologian: *Hymns of Divine Love,* op. cit., *Hymn* 24, p. 136.

9. Jacques Leclercq: *Christ and the Modern Conscience* (N.Y.: Sheed & Ward, 1962) tr. by R. Matthews, pp. 245-246.

10. Cited by André Loof in *Teach Us to Pray;* tr. H. Hoskins (Chicago: Franciscan Herald Press, 1974), pp. 38-39.

11. For a rather up-to-date presentation of this problem, with particular emphasis on the doctrine of St. Thomas Aquinas as compared with some modern theologians such as S.I. Dockx, K. Rahner, L. Von Rudloff, see: William J. Hill, O.P.: *Proper Relations to the Indwelling Divine Persons* (Wash. D.C.: The Thomist Press, 1956).

12. St. Symeon the New Theologian: *Traites Ethiques,* in: *Sources Chrétiennes Séries* (Paris: Cerf, 1967) Vol. 129, no. 11, 167-177; pp. 340-342.

13. Jan Ruysbroeck: *The Adornment of the Spiritual Marriage;* tr. C.C. Wynschenk Dom (London: J.M. Dent & Sons, LTD., 1916) p. 51.

14. Pseudo-Macarius: *Homily 33,* in: *Intoxicated with God,* tr. George A. Maloney, S.J. (Denville, N.J.: Dimension Bks., 1978) pp. 182-183.

15. St. Isaac of Nineveh: *Directions on Spiritual Training,* in: *Early Fathers from the Philokalia,* tr. E. Kakloubovsky and G. Palmer (London: Faber & Faber, 1954) pp. 243.

16. St. John of the Cross: *The Living Flame of Love,* in: *The Collected Works of St. John of the Cross,* tr. Kieran Kavanaugh, O.C.D. and Otilio Rodriguez, O.C.D. (Wash. D.C.: ICS Publications, 1963) p. 582.

Chapter Seven

1. This text, as George T. Montague, S.M. points out as the common consensus of modern scriptural exegetes, ". . . refers here not to the individual body of the Christian but to the Christian community as such," in: *The Holy Spirit: Growth of a Biblical Tradition,* (N.Y.: Paulist Press, 1976) p. 138.

2. cf.: Chapter Two of this book.

3. St. Thomas: *Summa Theologica,* pg. 151: no. 3: 1, q. XLIII.

4. B. Froget, O.P.: *The Indwelling of the Holy Spirit in the Souls of the Just* (N.Y.: Paulist Press, 1921) p. 130.

5. St. Gregory of Nazianzus: *Oratio 34,* 12; in LNPF, op. cit. p. 337.

6. St. Cyril of Alexandria: *Commentary on the Gospel of St. John, PG LXXIV,* 293.

7. Didymus the Blind: *De Spiritu Sancto,* n. 25; *PG XXXIX,* 1055-1056.

8. G.A. Maloney, S.J.: *Inward Stillness* (Denville, N.J.: Dimension Bks., 1976) p. 64.

9. St. Augustine: *In Psalmo,* PL XLIX, n. 2; PL 86, 565.

10. Peter De Rosa: *Come, Holy Spirit* (Milwaukee: Bruce Comp., 1968) p. 60.

Chapter Eight

1. Dr. Arthur Janov: "For Control, Cults Must Ease the Most Profound Pains," an article that appeared in *Los Angeles Times* (Dec. 10, 1978) part VI, 3 and was an excerpt from his forthcoming book, *Prisoners of Pain.* Harper & Row.

2. St. Gregory of Nyssa: *De Oratione Catech. Magna,* 37, in: *LNPF,* 2nd Series, Vol. 5, pp. 504-505.

3. Ibid., p. 506.

4. St. John Chrysostom: *Homilies on St. John's Gospel;* tr. Sr. Thomas Aquinas Goggin, S.C.H., in: *Fathers of the Church,* Vol. 33 (N.Y.: Fathers of the Church, Inc., 1957) pp. 468-469.

5. Pope Paul VI: *Ecclesiam Suam* (N.Y.: Paulist Press, 1965) p. 30.

6. An excellent treatment of the doctrine of St. Cyril of Alexandria on the image and likeness is found in W. Burghardt: *The Image of God in Man according to Cyril of Alexandria* (Wash. D.C.: Catholic Univ. of America Press, 1957).

7. St. Cyril of Alexandria: *Commentary on St. John's Gospel, PG* LXXIV, 553-561.

8. St. Hilary of Poitiers: *De Trinitate,* 15, *PL* XLII, 248.

9. Ibid., 14, *PL* X, 247.

10. St. Symeon the New Theologian: *Hymns of Divine Love,* Hymn 30 in: *Hymns of Divine Love,* tr. G.A. Maloney, S.J. (Denville, N.J.: Dimension Books, 1975) pp. 169-170.

11. M.V. Bernadot, O.P.: *From Holy Communion to the Blessed Trinity* (Westminster, Md.: The Newman Bookshop, 1947) p. 44.

12. M. Scheeben, op. cit., pp. 493-494.

13. Cited by Hugo Rahner, S.J.: "The Beginnings of the Devotion in Patristic Times," in: *Heart of the Savior,* ed. by Josef Stierli (N.Y.: Herder & Herder, 1957) p. 54.

14. Teilhard de Chardin: *Hymn of the Universe* (N.Y.: Harper & Row, 1965) p. 92.

15. W.B. Yeats and E.J. Ellis, eds.: The Works of William Blake (London, 1893), Vol. 1, p. 276.

16. T.S. Eliot: *Four Quartets* (N.Y.: Harcourt & Brace & Co., 1943) p. 39.

17.   St. Symeon the New Theologian: *Hymns of Divine Love,*
      tr. by G.A. Maloney, S.J., op. cit., *Hymn 52,* pp. 265-266.